D0677047

Labyrinth of Desire

Also by Rosemary Sullivan

Biography
By Heart: Elizabeth Smart/ A Life
Shadow Maker: The Life of Gwendolyn MacEwen
The Red Shoes: Margaret Atwood Starting Out

Poetry
The Space a Name Makes
Blue Panic
The Bone Ladder: New and Selected Poems

Literary Criticism
Theodore Roethke: The Garden Master
Learning to Make Fire: Selected Essays

Rosemary Sullivan

Labyrinth of Desire

Women, Passion, and Romantic Obsession

HarperFlamingoCanada

For information address
HarperCollins Publishers Ltd,
55 Avenue Road, Suite 2900,
Toronto, Ontario, Canada M5R 3L2

www.harpercanada.com

HarperCollins books may be purchased for
educational, business, or sales promotional
use. For information please write:
Special Markets Department,
HarperCollins Canada,
55 Avenue Road, Suite 2900,
Toronto, Ontario, Canada M5R 3L2

First HarperFlamingo edition

Canadian Cataloguing in Publication Data

Sullivan, Rosemary
Labyrinth of desire :
women, passion, and romantic obsession

Includes bibliographical references.
I S B N 0-00-255411-9

1. Women – Psychology.
2. Relationship addiction.
I. Title.

BF575.L8S78 2001   152.4'1'082
C00-932348-1

01 02 03 04 K R O 4 3 2 1

Printed and bound in Canada
Set in Weiss

For Laurie and Tara

Contents

Introduction

I have spent a good deal of time sitting in cafés with other women talking late into the night about romantic obsession. I can tell when the subject is coming up. The tone of our conversation changes. Our voices become intense and urgent and fall a few decibels so as not to be over-heard—confessions are to follow. Each of us feels an urgency to tell our own story. And almost everyone has a love story. The stories start the same way, usually unex-pectedly, and have the same trajectory of longing and then of loss. We try to make sense of our obsessions. They are so slippery, so elusive to us that only by confessing them to a listener can we pin them down, make them real. But we also feel a bit of embarrassment as we talk. We think women go on too much about roman-tic love, though secretly we believe few things are more fascinating than the old, irresistible question: Why do we love as we do?

From the outset, I should make it clear that I am talking about one particular kind of love: romantic, obsessive love, the hot thing we fall into, the love we're all expected to experience and that we call *true* love. Think of novels like *Wuthering Heights* and *Doctor Zhivago*, or films like *Casablanca* and *The English Patient*. Think of torch songs and the tango. What they have in common is this: two people obsessed with each other while all the ordinariness of life, its consolations and diversions, vanishes. Nothing will do but for the lovers to be with each other. Often the story ends tragically. The lovers part or they die, and the quotidian world takes over once again.

In literature and art, love is a myth we tell ourselves. By myth I mean not an invention or falsehood but rather a narrative that enfolds our deepest beliefs and longings. Love is the story we place above all others, the one we invest with the most value.

But love is difficult to talk about. Why does the English language have only one word for it? Love is too outlandish, too protean to be poured into a single word. Spanish and Italian, for instance, use different words to describe the love for persons and the love for objects. A person can be loved, but objects only please. Yet in English, one can love a man, a woman, a house, and a dog. Love is even a score in tennis meaning zero; it comes from the saying: "Do it for love; do it for nothing." In English, one must resort to adjectives: erotic love, platonic love, fraternal love, romantic love.

There is the added difficulty of how to discuss love without falling into the clichés that barnacle it like an encrusted rock. Shelves of bookstores are full of self-help manuals about love written by anthropologists, sociologists, psychologists, medical doctors: *Women Who Love Too Much; Men Are From Mars, Women Are From Venus; Intimate Strangers*. They tell us that love is a cultural construct based on social or biological conditioning. Or they pathologize love as an illness we must get over. In front of the overwhelming sensations of passion, they are largely irrelevant.

What interests me is romantic, obsessive love. How to talk about it? Perhaps I might begin by saying what I'm not talking about. I'm not talking about a love affair. That's a romantic interlude, expected by both lovers to be evanescent and looked back at with gentle affection and a tinge of nostalgia. I'm not talking about sensible love, the person selected as a good life partner. I'm not even talking about romance, which evokes red roses and Hallmark cards. When I speak of romantic love, I'm thinking hunger and longing, desperation and ecstasy.

My sense of romantic love inevitably involves obsession. It occurs when we meet the person we feel is essential for our life. Without that person, we will die. It happens when life stops us suddenly in our tracks and we love in a way that we didn't know was possible. Thinking/talking/dreaming/obsessing—life is suspended on the thread of one other human being.

The story of obsessive love is a story about wanting something so badly that we will risk everything to gain it. As we hurtle down the highway at break-neck speed to meet our lover, as we defy all prescriptions for rational behavior, we are living a drama, and nothing else in the world matters. The puzzle is how we attach such life-and-death intensity to our feelings for these persons, since, after the obsession has played itself out, often these same persons stand before us almost strangers.

What's it all about?

The seventeenth-century French courtier and pundit La Rochefoucauld suggested that we fall in love the way we do because we have learned it from literature. We long to live our lives as if they were the heroic love stories we script. But what actually happens when we attempt it?

For more than a decade now I have been nagged by a compulsion to write about this. Even while I was working on other books, this one sat in the back of my mind. Slowly, I started collecting stories of romantic obsession: stories from literature, stories told to me by friends including other writers, and stories from my own life. These are the sources on which I will draw for the conversation that follows.

I have come to believe that falling obsessively in love is

one of life's necessary assignments. It cracks us open. We put everything at risk. In the process we discover the dimensions of our own appetites and desires. And life, to be lived fully, demands desire. The experience is really an initiation, a process of transition; it is not a place to get stuck and is never a life solution.

In talking about these matters, it's so hard to avoid generalizations, and nothing is more individual than falling in love. So to conjure up what I mean by the hot thing, the messy thing, obsessive passion, I have decided to tell a love story. Like all love stories, it is half invention, half truth.

1

Women of the Heart

This story begins in a hotel room in the old historic center of Mexico City, a great beast of a city, ancient and potent, with a sacrificial temple and a wall of skulls at its excavated heart. To be precise, it begins at a window. It was one of those exceptional windows, a catalyst for longing: huge, opening a few feet from the floor by means of two iron handles. It opened naked, with no screen to protect from the outside.

She had come to Mexico looking for adventure. She'd felt paralyzed, stuck, as if her life had hit a wall. No space to breathe, to feel. She needed to get her life started again.

She took to standing at that window. It faced on to an ugly little courtyard surfaced in brick tile the color of the red earth of Mexico, with four tiny planters containing scraggly cacti and miniature desiccated palms. Someone had left a ladder straddled across one of the planters, though she never saw anyone out there. The courtyard ended abruptly in a wall of gray concrete, the kind of material usually reserved for the backsides of things, with a duct that snaked its way up to the sky. On the left she could see only the interior of a parking arcade and the occasional lights of cars slipping in and out of its dark corridors. But to the right, almost within her reach, there were high windows like hers.

The curtains were always drawn. Each day she would look at those windows and wonder whether there might be someone standing there, waiting in that adjacent room at midday. But the globe of light she saw was only a reflection of her own lamp. She would look up at the sky mottled by thick gray stains from the relentless pollution and think how absurd she was to be standing there expecting something romantic from an old hotel.

She had always wanted to live in a hotel. Writers lived in hotels. She had read about Jean-Paul Sartre and Simone de Beauvoir on Boulevard St. Germain coming down for sea urchins at four in the afternoon after a day's writing, while someone else cleaned the room. In a hotel you lived from a suitcase and moved on if the service wasn't good.

After a month she knew every inch of the Gran Hotel. It had once been an elegant department store, built when art deco finally arrived in the colonial capital. On each floor a balcony circled the empty center, and five floors above, a magnificent stained-glass roof arched overhead like some monstrous exotic flower. She felt like an insect scrambling around its stem. She imagined the ghosts of rich Mexican ladies sitting on elegant chairs as young girls paraded the latest fashions through its draperied rooms.

At four o'clock every afternoon she took to sitting in the hotel café to drink tequila and sangrita, watching the birds in their stained-glass cages catapulting at mad speeds among artificial branches. She tried to look as if she were waiting for some secret assignation.

Each day she set out to explore the city, visiting the tiny art galleries and museums hidden in its labyrinths. She should have been enjoying herself and, in a way, she was. But she felt oddly exposed. Lovers shouted from billboards and eyed her from their café tables as she paced her solitary walks.

It was raining one day the way it can only in Mexico— hot and thick, bringing the sky down with it. Instead of passing the Ex-Palacio Arzobispal, she stepped inside for shelter. The gallery was showing an exhibition called "Damas de Corazón." She was amused by the poster, an absurd graffito of a red heart with a little red hat meant to be a flame. It looked like an advertisement for a blood clinic. She noticed a young man staring at it, as if puzzled that this piece of anatomy should be stuck on a wall. Catching her looking at him, he smiled and remarked in English, "They make such a fuss about that muscle. It's only a pump, after all." She laughed, and then passed through the turnstile.

The museum was small, only five rooms. Each room contained a self-portrait by one of the damas de corazón along with a bizarre collection of objects that had once been central to the artist's life. One room was a bedroom with a wheelchair beside a four-poster hung with little dancing skeletons; another, a study containing a desk filled with pre-Colombian female torsos. Yet another was an elegant dining room, on its table a collection of eccentric mementos: a butterfly, a baby alligator, a wooden snake, a monkey with a barbed-wire mask menacing a bride doll. The walls in this room were covered with framed letters outlined with drawings of hearts. One drawing, called *Ruin*, was of a broken head with the inscription, "Everything for Nothing."

When she entered the next room, she almost staggered, so powerful was the attractive force of two particular paintings. The first was called *Lovers*. Two lovers were holding hands; the face of each was a mirror, and as they stared into each other's eyes, they were lost in their own reflections. Their passion was so intense that a whirl of steam rose from their matching blue clothes and condensed into water, drowning their feet. The space around them was mysterious, black and stippled with falling light.

The other painting was called *Farewell*. The lovers had separated and were just barely visible disappearing down adjacent corridors. But their shadows stretched back to take a last passionate kiss. That kiss squeezed her heart as she watched the shadows consume each other.

She was so absorbed that she didn't notice she was under scrutiny. The young man had followed her. She stopped abruptly to take him in. He must have been about thirty. He was not conventionally handsome. His head seemed slightly too large for his body. His face was a collection of disproportionate and almost awkward features. But composed, it had a certain grace. The most distinctive feature was his eyes: when he smiled, as he did now, they crinkled about the edges and warmed his whole face. There was nothing remarkable about the way he dressed—a simple striped shirt and jeans on his tall frame. Perhaps it was the black hair reaching to his shoulders that gave him a kind of seductive arrogance that she found pleasurable to look at.

She watched him with a mixture of attraction and unexpected trepidation. What was she afraid of, anyway? There was an undertow to the moment, a shock of recognition. She left the museum strangely confident he would follow. Aware he was watching, she intentionally dropped the brochure emblazoned with the red heart. She stooped from the waist to retrieve it, wanting to display her body, to be a beautiful artifact for his scrutiny. She meant her gesture to be a call. She sat down at a nearby sidewalk café and waited.

He made as if to pass casually and then came up to her

table. "I noticed you at the exhibition," he said. "May I sit down?" And then, as he settled himself into the seat, "You're American?"

"I'm from Thunder Bay," she replied.

"Ah, Canadian." She showed her surprise.

"Thunder Bay. Medicine Hat. Kicking Horse Pass. When I was a kid, those were magic destinations on my map. When I grew up I was going to go there."

"And did you?"

"No."

"You're from Mexico?"

"No."

"What brings you here?"

"I'm looking for another life."

He said his name was Varian, and he had been in Mexico for two years. Though his father was American and he'd grown up in California, his mother was Mexican. He had come to discover his mother's country.

He seemed to know everything about Mexican art. He dazzled her with stories of the damas de corazón, about all their scandals and love affairs. And then, tentatively, as if surprised by his own candor, he began to talk of his life. It was as though he was opening a suitcase, taking out a memory here, an anecdote there, and laying them carefully on the table.

"My mother was a beautiful woman," he said. "She was exotic but she was quite possibly mad. I never remember her wearing anything but white. She hated America and she hated me too."

"Why would you say that?" she asked.

"Because she did. Once, when I was a child, I was attacked by boys at school because I looked too Mexican. I remember racing home with blood running down my face. All she said was, 'Go clean up. You look ugly.' I was ten years old. I always believed I was ugly."

The way his eyes seemed to retreat like frightened animals as he said this reeled her in. Suddenly she was talking about herself too, about her family, and then about her desire to be a writer. She never talked about this. It was presumptuous, fraudulent, to pretend to be a writer when she'd written so little. Yet here she was telling him about the novel she wanted to write—a family saga about her grandmother, who'd been what was called a home child, one of the thousands of orphans the British government had shipped to Canada at the beginning of the century. An expedient way to clean up the slums. And children like her grandmother had ended up working as indentured servants.

"It's a moving story. You must write it," he said. "Everyone has a story. This is yours." The generosity of his total attention thrilled her. How was it possible to feel so immediately intimate with a complete stranger?

The world came alive as they sat there. She was aware of the sudden heat of his hand on her arm, his beautiful elongated fingers playing across her knuckles, the mixed odor of wet pavement and caramel and coffee, even a little hummingbird rarely seen in Mexico City—a chuparrosa, he called it—sucking the pink bougainvillea on the wall of the café. Then, abruptly, the conversation ended. He said he had to be somewhere. As he got up to leave, he asked for her phone number.

In the days that followed she haunted that section of the Zócalo, going there under any pretext. At the museum, she read every letter on the walls of the "Damas de Corazón." They began to know her at the Zapata café. The loneliness she felt was excruciating, yet somehow rich and operatic. Every noon she would take the long walk up to Chapultepec Park where a strange spectacle unfolded to which she was becoming addicted. It was called the Danza del Volador, the flyer's dance. It was an ancient ceremony. Five men climbed a wooden pole a hundred feet in height. While one of them stood on a hoop attached to the top and played a flute, the other four hung by their feet from ropes. As the hoop slowly turned, they descended head down to the ground. The rhythm of their circling was beautiful: relentless and hypnotic as the earth's gravitation pulled them to its surface. Submitting themselves to such a terrible descent was an act of worship. Even though she didn't understand the dance's ancient motive, it compelled her. That's how she felt: free-falling in a slow, hypnotic descent.

It was a week before she saw him again. He called at

last, suggesting they take a trip to the town of Guanajuato, where the artist Diego Rivera had been born. She was elated. She waited in her room for what seemed forever until he finally phoned from the lobby. She was eager to display him to the doorman, to the waiters and receptionists who had been witness to her loneliness over the past weeks. She glided with him through the lobby. He was her trophy. He had become that beautiful.

Why do we remember one thing rather than another? It was the bus ride to Guanajuato she would remember, speeding through the brilliant light in the High Sierras. It was as if the sun itself had become water and the bus was breaking through, while just beyond the window the unchanging waste of mesquite and chaparral spread for mile after mile. She couldn't take her eyes off his hands. She watched his fingers, the bones beneath his skin. She wanted this man. Afterwards she could always call back that image like a hologram: three-dimensional and palpable. Whenever some touch of light hit a landscape at a particular slant, she could recover exactly how her body had focused with the shock of desire.

Guanajuato seemed to sit in a bowl as they descended the deep gorge in the dusk. It was built like a labyrinth over a honeycomb of ancient tunnels. The bus approached the city through the tunnels underneath, as if entering a medieval time warp, and they emerged at its heart. They found a room in the Hotel Catedral, which had once served as the Prussian consulate. The room was chaste, like a nun's cell, with a bed in one corner covered with mosquito netting.

When they made love for the first time, his beauty startled her. He was lean and arrow-like, yet supple as water as his body engulfed hers. He had a seductive way of sliding his mouth towards hers and pulling back, his eyes like pinpricks of black light. She felt he was peeling back her skin layer by layer with his tongue. And the way he spread her legs before entering her made it a ceremony. Her legs trembled like stalks in wind as she came again and again. She was as high as she'd ever been.

"You're so good at this," he laughed.

She could feel his body shake as she lay curled along the curve of his spine. The room echoed with the shudders and incoherent cries of their lovemaking. When they finally left the hotel to stroll through the park, the smell of their sex filled the hot night air.

He said he wanted to take her to the Mummy Museum—she had to taste the candied skeletons. Built beside a graveyard, the museum fronted on to a plaza filled with vendors hawking handicrafts from their stalls. Papier-mâché skulls gaudily decorated with blue and green sequined eyes were piled in bins like strange fruit. They entered the museum's catacomb-like corridors. From upright and horizontal glass cases, perfectly preserved bodies stared back at them. Some wore boots or slippers and tatters of clothing. She was appalled. Their caved-in faces still carried the record of their death;

some were serene, others grotesquely deformed.

There were more than fifty of them—men, women, children, and infants. Varian said that most of the bodies had been exhumed in the nineteenth century. At that time, according to the local legend, a law required relatives to pay leases on graves. The deceased whose relatives were unable to pay were unceremoniously dug up and were found to be perfectly preserved—something to do with the chemical composition of the soil. "No tax relief for the dead in Mexico," he said with a laugh. "If you didn't pay, your grandfather got to be the local entertainment." As she looked at him, she was thinking that if their own two bodies were put in those museum cases, frozen in the act of making love, they would still be beautiful.

That night she dreamed she was walking in labyrinths, entering caves, finding hidden crypts. In the dream Varian offered her a sardine can filled with penises and asked her to choose one.

She awoke suddenly. All her boundaries were giving way. What was she doing in Mexico anyway?

She'd always thought of herself as a rather ordinary person, too ordinary for her own liking. Born at the end of a Catholic family of five children in Thunder Bay, a small city where the snow piled feet above her head every winter, she'd left as soon as she could. She'd needed to get away from her mother, who drank too much in order to drown out the absence of a traveling, philandering husband. She used to tell people she left home when she was three, the day she took her toys to play at a neighbor's house and asked to stay forever. Of course she was looking for love. Who isn't?

Varian was a painter. He invited her to his studio in an old palace on Insurgentes Avenue in a rundown section of the city. The courtyard staircase had once been elegant but was now tottering after too many earthquakes. She climbed to the fifth floor. He had only one room, mostly empty except for a bed in one corner, a card table and chair, a gas stove, and a sink filled with unwashed dishes. But the walls were covered with his paintings. They all had the same title: *The Itinerary of a Naked I.* Each painting depicted a figure—sometimes male, sometimes female—standing in a corner, shoulders hunched, about to walk into an empty landscape. Some were red, others blue, green, yellow. The monotony was overwhelming, as if they were stuck. She felt that in the recesses of his mind she was looking into the mirror of her own loneliness. As they sat at his card table drinking tequila, he began to speak of his family. His story caught her off guard.

"It was the war that did it," he said. "They could never recover that happiness. My father was eighteen when he went to war, not as a soldier but as secretary to an American called Varian Fry—thus my name. Fry had been sent to France in 1940 by the Emergency Rescue Committee, a group organized in New York to liberate all the leading intellectuals and artists when the Nazis occupied the country. He arrived with $3,000 strapped to his leg, my father in tow, and a list of people he intended to save. He and my father set up shop in a house called Villa Air-Bel in Marseilles. They claimed to have saved a thousand of the cream of the European crop. My father had a wonderful time: all those artists and philosophers. They were crazy with fear and they partied endlessly. He met my mother there, a young Mexican artist stranded in France."

"It must have been terrifying," she said, "all of them waiting to escape."

"No, no, it was like living in a film. Because they got out, it was romantic. My father loved to tell these stories. There was even a psychopathic fisherman, a guy who was supposed to be rescuing them. My father had bribed him to take them to Casablanca, but luckily their money was stolen and they missed the boat. It turned out fourteen of his passengers were buried in his backyard. My mother was disappointed in America. She always longed for the old days in France. My arrival was an accident. She stopped painting, and it was my fault. Eventually she stopped doing anything. You can spend a lifetime making up for stuff like that."

She was disconcerted by the knife-edge of bitterness in his voice, yet she was moved by the depth of his hurt. She wanted to soothe him, to tell him that not everyone betrayed.

Mostly they went to his studio where they made love, and then they walked the city. He always knew which streets had elegant mansions with colonial frescoes, which anonymous door to slip past into an elegant court-yard with walls covered in revolutionary murals, or which tiny church held devotional retablos dedicated to the Virgin of close escapes.

One night he invited her to a farewell party for his art teacher at the Zapata café. Festive piñatas hung from the ceiling, and a mariachi band traveled from table to table. This was the first time she'd seen him with other people, and she was surprised at how distressed she was to share him. She was almost disconcerted to discover he had a life.

He was very charismatic. She read the room. The way certain women watched him, she could begin to imagine his history, drawing lines between him and the women who circled. He soon seemed to her like Gulliver tacked down by endless strings. One woman in particular unnerved her, greeting Varian as though publicly staking a claim.

Varian immediately steered her in the direction of a table at the back. "You must meet Professor Martinez," he said. Propped up in a stiff black suit, Professor Martinez was tied to the chair. His wide-open eyes stared unflinch-ingly into the room. He was dead. The others were sitting around the table toasting him with their sangritas. "He wanted to be at his own party just once, after he died," Varian said, laughing at her obvious shock. "Ah, my little Canadian."

Later that night, as they lay making love in his studio bed, she heard a key turn in the door. The woman who'd so obviously claimed him at the party entered carrying two oranges. When she saw the two of them, she set down the oranges carefully: "I should have known I would need to bring three," she said. "Let me see her." Exasperated, Varian threw back the covers, exposing their naked bodies. The woman gave a startled cry and fled. Turning back towards her half-apologetically, Varian climbed out of the bed and followed. There was shouting in the hallway and then the woman was gone.

She was surprised that, instead of being angry, she was aroused. She felt as though she'd woken up in a French film. When Varian returned she said, almost coyly, "You shouldn't have done that."

"Done what?" he asked. His voice was a knife cutting through ice.

"Pulled the sheet back."

Giving her a look of such contempt that it startled her, he grabbed his clothes and marched out. The cruelty of that look almost effaced her. The world reeled. She suddenly had no ballast. There was nothing to hold on to.

Within fifteen minutes he was back. He said he'd gone out to buy cigarettes. And then, with no further reference to what had occurred, he told her of the dream he'd had earlier, before the woman intruded. He was standing outside an apartment house in an abandoned city. A man invited him inside. As he wandered from room to room, a strange carnival was under way. He was led to a woman sitting serenely like a Buddha, but when the woman's cloak fell away, she had two rows of little breasts that ended not in nipples but in bird beaks. Next he found himself in a room where a woman was dressing. She said she was the dream catcher and that if he changed quickly enough he could live in the dream time. But he was not able to take off his clothes. And then the apartment disappeared, and he was standing alone in the street.

His dream reeled her in tighter. What had it to do with her? Did he see her as the dream catcher who could help him to change? Was this some kind of appeal? Clearly he felt compelled by her if he could offer her these broken shards of his life.

Yet, after that night, she began to intuit that something had changed. As if they'd reached an apex of some sort, and now the momentum would be downward. At times she found herself walking aimlessly through the streets of Mexico. It was the most exciting city in the world, and yet for her it now had the indecipherable vagueness of a dream. At moments, the whole affair seemed ridiculous— dead men in cafés, women with oranges. She felt as though she were participating in some kind of dress rehearsal. There was something she was trying to get right. But what?

Sometimes, bewildered, she would wander into the cathedral in the Zócalo and sit in the chapel of the Black Christ. It had always intrigued her, the idea of a black Christ. At first she had thought it a moving sign of the imperial church's effort to honor the local people. But the legend told a different story: the statue had once been white, but the bishop's servant, who hated him, put belladonna on its feet so that when the bishop bent to kiss them as he did every day, the poison would kill him. The Christ figure had absorbed the poison and turned black. How else could Christ be black in this country except by treachery? In Mexico, there was always a story with treachery at its heart.

Everything's treacherous, she thought. Varian was treacherous. She could never quite pin him down, never quite fix him in her mind. It became clear he was still seeing the lady of the oranges, as she took to calling her. The woman had held on to the key to his flat.

With no one to talk to, she felt trapped in endless circles in her own mind. "*That* kind of love," she would have told her friend Janet. "Love as a code language." They would have laughed and known what they were laughing about, even though they couldn't name it. They would have dragged out the old clichés: "It's just that men are such a mystery, they're another species; what do they want? We women are love addicts." At least in talking she might have recovered her equilibrium. Instead, she had a sensation of being suspended in a net.

She tried confronting him. She had been willing to risk everything, she pleaded. He said he couldn't choose. He walked out in disgust.

Her pain filled all of Mexico City. She had been sliced open. Alone in her hotel room, she found herself bellowing like an animal. A piece of her was being ripped out. She let it happen.

How could he make light of everything? Sneer even at what he called "this entanglement"? How could she have been so wrong about so much? She thought she had known him, but who was this stranger? They had been in love, she was sure of that, but gradually he had closed over, sealed himself up. He had lost his nerve. That was it. No words could penetrate now to make things right. She felt she could be in this limbo forever. How did it ever end? Did one person just get exhausted?

One day she found herself boarding a plane for Toronto. Back at home, she tended herself like a wound. What had that been about? she wondered. Lying on the mattress that served as a bed in her dingy apartment, she felt her life shrivel. Through the open windows she heard traffic; feet heading to work, streetcars creaking to a stop, cars speeding on. She hated the world with its calm assurance of purpose. It was all a ruin. She had staked everything. Everything for Nothing.

2

The Story
Beneath the Story

No single story can stand for all stories, but most of us, in some way or another, have lived a version of this one. It begins with such elation, an encounter that promises everything because the person has touched some spring that opens the box of ourselves. Ah yes, that lovely stage of spreading things out for each other: anecdotes, jokes, intimacies, and two lives suddenly enfold and match. Everything is soon colored by our obsession with the other person; everything is filtered through the exquisite inflation of passion.

But then the illusion of mutuality is shattered. Some misunderstanding, some missed cue, some pressing other life intrudes. And the alternative kind of obsession takes over. The passive waiting through long empty nights as time dissolves, empties, and ceases to be real. The long, hopeful letters crafted so carefully to achieve the right tone. And possibly never sent. The conversations with confidantes as we try to understand. There is always the hope that exactly the right words, if discovered, can resolve the confusion. The miserable rituals of obsession.

And when the experience is devastating enough, it can be deeply damaging. Resolving never to be hurt like this again, a person can seal over, shut down, and some capacity for love and trust will die. I have a friend who, having had her heart broken, snaps at me whenever the subject of romantic obsession comes up.

But there is no reason to be cynical. In these encounters, something much more important is going on than a failed love affair. In fact, there is another story lying just beneath the ostensible story. It has nothing to do with the other person but has everything to do with oneself. In the following pages, I will attempt to decode my story of romantic obsession, to explore what it is we are experiencing when we fall obsessively in love.

3

The Empty Landsc

She had come to Mexico looking for adventure. She'd felt para-
lyzed, stuck, as if her life had hit a wall. No space to breathe,
to feel. She needed to get her life started again.

Perhaps the place to begin is to ask why we seldom talk
about the preconditions for "falling in love." By that I
mean the state of mind that precedes it. Most people who
fall obsessively in love claim that it happens precipi-
tously, unexpectedly. But the kind of obsession that
rushes in like a firestorm usually occurs either when we
are young and want to get our lives started or when our
lives get stuck and we need to jump-start them again. We
are rarely self-aware enough to realize how we participate
in our own fantasies or to decipher the roles we play. And
so of course we do not always recognize when we are
searching for our invented lover.

But I believe there's almost always a prerequisite.

.ove in this way will usually occur at a time of
.on. We may not be conscious of it, but something
, ended and something new must begin. Romantic
obsession is a cataclysm breaking up the empty landscape. Like a strange exotic plant, it grows in arid soil.

How many dead marriages end with one partner falling
madly for someone else? It is a way out. I think of a
passage from one of my favorite novels, Gustave
Flaubert's *Madame Bovary*, published in 1857. Emma
Bovary, a doctor's wife in a provincial town in Normandy,
suddenly recognizes that she has fallen in love:

> But, when she looked in the mirror, she was startled
> by her own face. Never had she had eyes so large, so
> dark, so mysterious. Something subtle, transfiguring,
> was surging through her.
>
> She kept saying to herself: "I have a lover! A lover!",
> savouring this idea. ... At last, she was to know the
> pleasures of love, that fever of happiness which she
> had despaired of. She was entering something
> marvelous where everything would be passion,
> ecstasy, delirium; blue immensity was all about her;
> the great summits of sentiment glittered in her mind's
> eye, ordinary existence appeared far below in the
> distance, in shadow, in the gaps between these peaks.
>
> She summoned the heroines from the books she
> had read, and the lyric host of these unchaste women
> began their chorus in her memory, sister-voices,

enticing her. She merged into her own imaginings, playing a real part, realizing the long dream of her youth, seeing herself as one of those great lovers she had so long envied. Indeed, Emma felt the satisfaction of revenge. Had she not suffered enough? This was her moment of triumph, and love, so long sealed in, poured out in a copious fizzing rush. She savoured it without remorse, without anxiety, without worry.

Flaubert is being sardonic, of course, and at Emma Bovary's expense. But he is also sympathetic. In her tiny little bourgeois life, Emma is longing for something larger. Literature has told her it will be love.

And Emma is right about the "unchaste" heroines singing in her memory. Most of the great love stories are about adulterous passion. Think of *Tristan and Iseult, Launcelot and Guinevere, Anna Karenina, Wuthering Heights,* or such twentieth-century masterpieces as *Doctor Zhivago, The English Patient, Casablanca,* and *The End of the Affair.* In each one of these stories, there is a profound impediment that keeps the lovers apart and heightens the intensity and price of passion. Without obstacles there can be no obsession. The obstacle is a husband or a wife.

Emma is also right about something else. Love will crack her open, will be the route to feeling those large emotions that lay as yet untouched. But it is dangerous because once those emotions are unleashed, everything changes. There is no going back.

Like Emma, the young woman in my story has the imagination to want a larger life. Alone she goes to an exotic place, which itself takes some courage. There she can act out any fantasy with impunity. (For the traveler, social proscriptions are relaxed. No one is watching.) She thinks she has come to Mexico to try to write her novel, but she is also secretly looking for love. Were it merely a romantic interlude she wanted, she could be light-hearted. There would be no obsession. But she needs to fill an emptiness, a sense of radical insufficiency within. She is desperate to get her life started. She is really searching for herself.

4

Love at First Sight

She watched him with a mixture of attraction and unexpected trepidation. What was she afraid of, anyway? There was an undertow to the moment, a shock of recognition.

The myths we attach to that first encounter are patently ridiculous. *Love at first sight*. How could love happen at a glance?

Yet love at first sight is a myth of the oldest vintage. The thirteenth-century author of *The Divine Comedy*, Dante Alighieri, was one of the first to describe it. He writes with panache in the florid style of his time, and one asks, as one always does with a writer, is it the language or the lady he is in love with?

Nine times the heaven of the light had revolved in its own movement since my birth and had almost returned to the same point when the woman whom my mind beholds in glory first appeared before my eyes. She was called Beatrice by many who did not know what it meant to call her this. ... She was dressed in a very noble colour, a decorous and delicate crimson, tied with a girdle and trimmed in a manner suited to her tender age. The moment I saw her I say in all truth that the vital spirit, which dwells in the inmost depths of the heart, began to tremble so violently that I felt the vibration alarmingly in all my pulses, even the weakest of them. As it trembled, it uttered these words: *Behold a god more powerful than I who comes to rule over me.*

At the time of this encounter, both Dante and Beatrice were nine years old. He never really knew her. She married a prominent Florentine banker and died in 1290 at the age of twenty-four. His grief at her death, and his dedication to her memory, is the stuff of legend. She remained his ideal, the woman who would guide him through paradise in his great poem *Paradiso*.

Whereas Dante only looked, others acted on their passions. In March 1912, D.H. Lawrence went to lunch at the home of his former professor Ernest Weekley. He was hoping for a job. There he met Weekley's wife, Frieda. Lawrence went home and wrote her a letter with the single line: "You are the most wonderful woman in all England." It was love at first sight. He knew immediately that she was the woman for him. He also knew that he could get her. They eloped that May and married two years later, and their marriage lasted through every conceivable storm and fracture until Lawrence's death in 1930 at the age of forty-five. Lawrence never lost his obsession for Frieda. She was his muse.

My own father's account of his meeting with my mother was a story of love at first sight. When I was a child I used to ask him to tell me the story over and over, even though I knew its every detail. A young soldier at the time, my father had fallen in love with a beautiful woman at a canteen dance. He lost her phone number and couldn't find her again. Three years later, he met her on a blind date. The point of his story was that he and my mother were fated to meet. Though there was much unhappiness in their marriage, my father never gave up his illusion that few men had loved with such intensity.

Perhaps I inherited my father's romanticism, because the first time I became obsessively involved I followed his model. My first contact with the man who would become my lover was hearing his voice on a long-distance telephone call. It was warm, playful, and seductive. And when I first saw him I fell head over heels. He was the perfect image of the male fantasy I had been carrying in my head.

Such stories, of course, don't apply to everyone. In fact, perhaps they apply only to those who, unwittingly, are primed to embark on a romantic obsession. For them, love at a glance has a psychological truth. The moment comes with a shock of recognition that leaves them breathless with surprise. Why this happens has nothing to do with fate or magic.

For the young writer like Lawrence or Dante, the lover is the muse, the catalyst to his own creativity. This is what makes her so dramatic, so gigantic. Suddenly she carries the load of all his desires. When we fall in love at a glance, the question we should ask ourselves (and this would apply to both men and women) is, What is it that we long for? Or perhaps, What are we lacking so that we can turn life in the direction we want? Creativity? Confidence? Authority? Recklessness? Irresponsibility? Or even darkness? Perhaps the lover is the outlaw in ourselves we don't quite have the nerve to claim.

After I talked with a friend about this peculiarity—that we have first to encounter ourselves in another before we can recognize ourselves—she dug out a diary she had kept when she was fifteen.

"This is where it begins," she said. "April 11, 1974. I saw Brian in the caf. How can I tell him I love him? God knows I want to. Oh I wish I had something to offer him. Brian, I only know when I'm near you I become at a loss for words. Oh why doesn't anything ever go my way?"

We laugh, it's so poignant. The adolescent crush, that craving, all-embracing infatuation that consumes, the I'll-die-if-I-can't-know-him kind of obsession that can last for months or years. Brian was a phantom, an invention from all the pop love songs my friend knew by heart and whose words ringed the margins of her diary.

And I think back to those songs she was hearing and the mostly male teen idols who sang them. Who didn't want to be on the receiving end of all that male desire? Yet how infantilizing those lyrics were—a Barbie doll version of the child-woman. One of the most popular was Bobby Vinton's banal "Roses Are Red," lifted from the rhyme,

> Roses are red,
> Violets are blue,
> Sugar is sweet,
> And so are you.

In those days, young girls were being taught that it was dangerous to reveal themselves. Better to cut out the dark bits. Better to pretend to be as sweet as the male image of girls demanded. But what was actually going on in young girls' heads was much more seductive. I remember my own adolescence.

Working for a babysitting agency was the only way the females in my family could make any money, and we all babysat. Alone at night in strangers' houses (so sophisticated in my fourteen-year-old eyes because they all had basement rec rooms), I would turn on the stereo. I particularly loved the records of the jazz musician Al Hirt, with his smoky, seductive trumpet. While I sipped whatever sweet, sticky liquor I could find in the liquor cabinet, I would mime the words of "Fly Me to the Moon." Sometimes there would be copies of *Playboy* in those rec rooms, and, appalled and titillated, I scrutinized the female bodies and wondered what it would be like to be seen by a man. I had a crush on a leather-jacketed character with a ducktail who rode a motorcycle into the schoolyard as though he were James Dean. What would it be like to be seen by him? Of course, I'd never spoken two words to him.

Both my friend and I were typical young girls. How vulnerable and unworthy we felt in relation to the phantoms we longed for. We were desperate to discover a sense of our own power, and we knew somehow that it lay in the mystery of sexuality. All we really wanted was to kick free of childhood and enter the dramatic and tantalizing adult world of sex. But we had to remain passive. The rule was that a girl was not allowed to initiate anything. She had to wait to be noticed.

Still, the story of adolescent longing is not the only story that was going on in my friend's diary. "If I ever get to know Brian I'll give him the new horse I'm drawing today, if it turns out." In the margin she added: "I just finished it! I like it. If I can ever get to know Brian 'well' I will give it to him or one of my best pictures." The drawing was dedicated to the "betterance" of her friendship with Brian.

My friend became a painter. Brian was her first fantasy

of the Other who would recognize *her*—who would acknowledge the valued and secret self she offered. He was her first muse. She never did speak to Brian, but that wasn't important. What mattered was that the unknown, unfathomable Brian about whom her feelings ran so deep was the route to a dramatic version of herself.

For the woman in my story, the lover is a vicarious route to some essential part of herself that she does not yet fully recognize or understand. For her, falling in love happens so quickly because this is not just any man. It is a lover in a particular context that she needs. He is the heroic territory she longs to occupy. *At a glance*, she is making a judgment: the lover can receive the projection of all that she longs for but that still lies unclaimed in herself.

5

The Dinner Party

Two lovers were holding hands; the face of each was a mirror, and as they stared into each other's eyes, they were lost in their own reflections. Their passion was so intense that a whirl of steam rose from their matching blue clothes and condensed into water, drowning their feet. The space around them was mysterious, black and stippled with falling light.

At a dinner party held in the fourth century B.C., the Greek playwright Aristophanes was asked to account for the love between human beings.

The first human creatures, he said, were shaped like eggs, with rounded backs and sides, four arms and four legs, and two heads on a cylindrical neck. They walked erect, backwards and forwards, but when they ran they looked like great colorful disks whirling in cartwheels over the earth. Fearing their power, the gods divided them in half, splitting them into separate entities, then turned their appendages around to face one way and tied everything together at the navel. Still halved and incomplete, we human creatures are eternally seeking our matching other halves.

Aristophanes added this important elaboration. The original creatures were all male, all female or hermaphrodite. Split in two, each part seeks its original other, thus accounting for homosexual and heterosexual love.

Aristophanes was a comic playwright, and there is something magnificently ridiculous about his eggs. Still, he touched the nerve center of obsession and yearning in love. Imagine the pain of these creatures who, having once had eyes both back and front, were made lonely, made achingly vulnerable by that dark space at the back of the head.

Love is a necessary obsession. But is it another we are searching for, or the missing half of ourselves?

6

The Shadow Artist

She had always wanted to live in a hotel. Writers lived in hotels. She had read about Jean-Paul Sartre and Simone de Beauvoir on Boulevard St. Germain coming down for sea urchins at four in the afternoon after a day's writing, while someone else cleaned the room.

The young woman in my story is making the mistake so many women make. She thinks that literature is life. She has romanticized the love stories she has read or heard and she wants to be in them. She is looking for the artist to fall in love with. Like I did when I was twenty-one. I married a poet, when what I truly wanted was to be a poet myself. I didn't know that I was setting myself up for romantic disaster.

This phenomenon among women is so familiar that it has even garnered a name: the shadow artist. In love with art but feeling inadequate and fearful of failure, or simply unable to find their own way, women have notoriously attached themselves to male artists. Sadly, they often end up settling for vicarious fulfillment of their own talent.

It's an old story. The women become appendages to what they think are epic lives, assuming the role of groupies, no less in high than in popular art. Plenty of men have boasted of their artistic harems, from Picasso and Henry Miller to Mick Jagger and Leonard Cohen. Artistic success always glows with a sexual aura. A famous poet once remarked to me, "What do I have to attract women but my genius?"

For my story I selected Jean-Paul Sartre and Simone de Beauvoir as the models my young protagonist aspires to. When I was a student visiting Paris, I experienced the thrill of seeing those two writers sitting in the Café Dôme eating sea urchins. In those days they were the ideal literary couple, she as impressive as he. Pretending to go to the washroom, I slipped past them several times. I wanted to feel the brush of greatness.

Two decades later, I read Deirdre Bair's biography of Beauvoir. Though rumors had been circulating for years, it was a terrible blow to discover how totally this pioneer of modern feminism had subordinated her talent to Sartre's demands.

The awful thing about biographies is that they often shatter the myths we make of writers' lives. From the time Beauvoir met Sartre at the Ecole Normale Supérieure in Paris when she was twenty-one, she fell under the spell of his verbal seduction. An acquaintance, Colette Audry, claimed that Sartre was voracious. He "seduced and conquered young girls by explaining their souls to them." And he *was* brilliant. He had shocked his fellow students by insisting, in all sincerity, that his ambition was "to become the man who knew the most about everything in the world that could be known." Beauvoir would say: "I was intelligent, certainly, but Sartre was a genius." All those who knew Sartre in his student days remarked on the feeling of being privileged in the presence of genius.

Sartre and Beauvoir became a powerful couple, but soon being his lover included becoming his pander, the go-between in his other love affairs. When she was a young teacher at the Lycée Jeanne d'Arc in Rouen north of Paris, Beauvoir turned over to Sartre the young women who had attached themselves to her as her disciples, and they became his lovers. These girls were "annexed," as she put it. He also took pleasure in describing the women he slept with in lurid details in his letters to Beauvoir. She was meant to share his triumph. The letters always ended with expressions of his superior love for her. She was the intellectual confidante he could not live without. Thus Sartre made her what her biographer calls the "third person in his bed." His trick was to build her up intellectually while he undermined her sexually.

At the age of sixty, Sartre adopted his young mistress, Arlette Elkaïm, rather than marry her. One of Sartre's biographers, Ronald Hayman, describes this most bizarre event in their life-long relationship as an act of aggression against Beauvoir, whose reward for "a lifetime of devotion" was to see her youngest rival given "unchallengeable ownership of everything Sartre had written, everything he possessed." Other biographers have suggested Sartre was simply feeling old—he is reported to have said to Arlette, "I'm not so good in bed anymore." It was also a practical decision. Arlette was an Algerian Jew, and by adopting her, Sartre was giving her French citizenship. The problem was that, having always avoided conflict with women, Sartre neglected to tell Beauvoir.

When she found out, she was devastated. How could she give up the Sartre/Beauvoir couple she presented to the world? Theirs was meant to be the ideal relationship. She had always said: *We are one person.* According to her, the unique privilege of her life was that she was "in perpetual dialogue with someone remarkable." Pretending nothing had changed, she therefore continued to accompany Sartre to meetings and conferences, and explained to the press that he had adopted Arlette for convenience, since she would be his literary executor. Only close friends knew the truth: that Arlette was Sartre's mistress.

Initially, the charade was easy to perpetuate. Sartre's "daughter" continued to give pride of place to Beauvoir, quietly deferring to her whenever Sartre and the two women appeared in public. Bair writes: "Sartre had Arlette and his other women, and his weekly rotation among them."

The civility between Beauvoir and Arlette did not survive Sartre's death. Three days after his cremation, Beauvoir learned that Arlette had emptied his apartment, afraid someone might steal Sartre's papers. It was a direct affront, since the only other person with a key to the apartment was Beauvoir. The real issue was who had the right to publish Sartre's manuscripts and letters. Beauvoir took a taxi to Arlette's apartment and humbled herself to plead for the manuscript *"Cahiers pour une morale"* that Sartre had said would be hers. According to Beauvoir, Arlette replied simply, "Ah, no, I don't think so."

The spectacle of Beauvoir and Arlette fighting over the literary remains of Jean-Paul Sartre would be grotesque were it not so pathetic. The manuscripts seemed almost more important to the women than the man who wrote them. Perhaps they were a source of intellectual valida-tion. Having lost control over Sartre's manuscripts, Beau-voir remarked: "That was when I knew that Sartre was really gone. That was when I accepted that what was real, the best part of my life, was over."

At Simone de Beauvoir's own death, the cortège of mourners who followed her casket through the streets of Paris numbered in the thousands. By writing *The Second Sex* she had changed forever the way women saw them-selves, and they loved her for it. But she hadn't even begun to deal with the patterns of her own life. She had taken second place, allowing herself to be defined by Sartre's needs and desires. As her biographer remarks, she had invested everything in Sartre, and "when he wasn't with her she felt herself less than nothing."

Why did the power dynamic work this way? Clearly, more than half a century ago, it was exceedingly hard for a woman to claim intellectual authority. Beauvoir had had to fight: first, her own family in order to get to university and study philosophy; then, the publishing establishment. In 1938, when she submitted her first novel, *When Things of the Spirit Come First,* to the publisher Gallimard, it was rejected. According to Sartre, Gallimard "were not yet ready to deal with what women thought and felt and wanted ... to publish such a book would brand them a subversive publishing house and they couldn't risk offending all sorts of patrons and critics." Privately, he gave her much needed support, telling her the novel was good and that she must believe in herself. Still, he also asked her not to make a fuss since it would reflect badly on himself, and he might need Gallimard for his own next book. He managed to soothe *and* to control.

How could she be so readily manipulated? We fail to account for how much our insecurity is filtered through what we believe others think of us. If Beauvoir felt her mind was not quite good enough, neither was her body. She read the fashion bible *Marie Claire* to improve her gaucheness—slimming those too fat hips with drapery. Meanwhile, Sartre, less than five feet tall and one of the ugliest men in the world, moved from lover to lover. It is appalling to think just how deep the damage went that it could sabotage a woman as brilliant as Simone de Beauvoir.

While never doubting that Sartre merited her unflinching devotion, a few years before her death at the age of seventy-eight, Beauvoir began to examine herself more scrupulously:

> I was a "token" woman for so many years. At home I was taught that girls were inferior to men even while I was told to behave like one; I went to schools where girls were given textbooks exhorting them to think like a man. My father praised me for having the brain of a man. I had a privileged situation with Sartre. And then there I was in 1956–57, writing my memoirs and praising myself for combining "a woman's heart and a man's brain," believing at the same time I was not renouncing my "femininity." No wonder I had to spend so much time thinking and writing about myself, who and what I was.

Beauvoir accomplished a great deal, achieving work of lasting importance independent of Sartre. Ironically, it never seems to have occurred to her that her contribution to her generation might even turn out to be more revolutionary than Sartre's; that with what she called her self-obsession, she would change the course of women's history.

*

The Beauvoir/Sartre story brings me to another point. Men have been able use their erotic relationships with women as a route to their own creativity. Indeed, falling in love has always seemed to be the male artist's first assignment. I think of Leonard Cohen's *Let Us Compare Mythologies*, written when he was twenty-two. Or of the Chilean poet Pablo Neruda's exquisite *Twenty Poems of Love and a Song of Despair*, written when he was twenty. "Ah, let me remember you as you were then, before you were," he implores. Readers have spent years speculating over the identities of the women addressed in the poems, but I would guess that Neruda and Cohen were as much in love with their own awakening power over language as with the young women who inspired it.

Many male artists have understood that muses exist solely to provide inspiration. The young women who assume that role cannot sustain it indefinitely. What these men want from the young women is awe. But women often seem not to grasp this. They believe they can make themselves indispensable and irreplaceable, and that this will somehow fulfill them. More often, though, like Beauvoir, they must watch the demoralizing parade of younger women, each in turn assuming the role of muse, while they themselves retreat to the background.

And why have women been willing to play muse? Perhaps it is easier to believe in someone other than yourself; easier to accept someone else's failures; easier to stand firm in defense of someone else's rights. Even easier to fast-track through another's success, rather than achieving your own. Eventually, however, you discover that you have nurtured in another what you should have nurtured in yourself and you are left empty. Even damaged. Bending your will to his, you lose your own passions and dreams.

Of course it's possible that, today, expectations have changed completely. Yet I doubt it. I have a friend who is a recording engineer and owns a sound studio. Fascinated by the collection of people who pass through, I often visit. One day a group calling itself Blue Bottle came to record a demo. Seven young men, their entourage, and their instruments arrived in a swarm with an energy that almost lifted the building from its foundation. They had roots from all over—Chile, Guyana, Egypt, Calgary, Mississauga. All shapes and sizes and colors, they seemed to me indiscriminately beautiful.

They were raw and confident. They knew they would make it, and their delight in their own possibilities attracted people to them as inevitably as flies to flypaper. Already in their entourage were three girls. Tribally costumed, with Cleopatra clipped hair and punk ankle boots, they too were exquisite. I almost wanted to cry out, the look on their faces was so worshipful—not so much of the young men themselves as of the energy generated by them. One girl basked in the glow, and in her arms the baby she carried basked too—a child in a child's arms.

In the lounge, four of the Blue Bottles sat before the television waiting their turn to record. They were watching the fashion channel, mesmerized by the costumed models and the high-tech glitz. This was the world to which they aspired. To my amazement, these young men knew the names of the designers and their models. They picked out the women they liked best. And one of the boys remarked, "Someday, she's going to be my groupie."

7

Erotic Gestures

Aware he was watching, she intentionally dropped the brochure emblazoned with the red heart. She stooped from the waist to retrieve it, wanting to display her body, to be a beautiful artifact for his scrutiny. She meant her gesture to be a call.

There's a curious somnambulism to the early stages of an obsessive love affair, as if we were hypnotized. We find ourselves doing things that are out of character, yet we feel compelled to do them as though directed by imperatives from within. My young woman wants the man's attention. And, with her provocative gesture, she sets out to get it. Later, however, she will not want to acknowledge her part in making this affair happen. She will prefer the conventional narrative: that lovers are fated to meet.

The gestural language that begins a love affair already defines the kind of affair it will be. I hold in my mind an image from one of my favorite films, Alfred Hitchcock's version of Daphne du Maurier's murder mystery *Rebecca*. Devotees of Hitchcock remember the powerful opening scene. The camera follows a road through a wooded, fog-filled landscape and stops abruptly at iron gates. The hypnotic voice of Joan Fontaine recounts a dream. The words we hear are taken almost verbatim from du Maurier's novel, which begins:

Last night I dreamt I went to Manderley again. It seemed to me I stood by the iron gate leading to the drive, and for a while I could not enter for the way was barred to me. ...

Then, like all dreamers, I was possessed of a sudden with supernatural powers and passed like a spirit through the barrier before me. The drive wound away in front of me, twisting and turning as it had always done, but as I advanced, I was aware that a change had come upon it. ... Nature had come into her own again and, little by little, in her stealthy, insidious way, had encroached upon the drive with long, tenacious fingers. ...

Moonlight can play odd tricks upon the fancy, even upon a dreamer's fancy. As I stood there, hushed and still, I could swear that the house was not an empty shell but lived and breathed as it had lived before. ... A cloud, hitherto unseen, came upon the moon, and hovered an instant like a dark hand before a face. The illusion went with it. ... I looked upon a desolate shell. ... We can never go back again.

The novel is not really a murder mystery but a love story. And even more interesting than the love story itself are the portraits of three women, the dead wife, her maid, and the new wife, all pitted against each other in a ruthless battle for supremacy. We never see the beautiful, narcissistic, adulterous Rebecca de Winter, except in a painting, yet her mysterious death drives the plot. Mrs. Danvers, the spinster housekeeper, ghost-like with her parchment white face and skeletal frame, is determined to destroy any young woman presumptuous enough to attempt to replace her dead mistress. And finally there is the second Mrs. de Winter (played by Joan Fontaine), seemingly demure and plain but, in fact, the strongest of the three. High-minded and virtuous, she will dissemble and lie to protect the stiff and domineering Maxim de Winter, who is the prime suspect in his wife's murder and the man she loves. In his early forties, he is played by a paternal, slightly graying, but exceedingly dashing Laurence Olivier.

The gesture I have in mind occurs very early in the film. The soon-to-be second Mrs. de Winter, an ingénue in her early twenties whose name we never learn, has seen Maxim de Winter exactly twice, and has already set her mind on him. As she enters the restaurant of the Princess Hotel in Monte Carlo where she is staying as a paid companion to a tiresome old woman, she notes his presence. We don't see him, but we watch her eyes turn momentarily to one side of the restaurant and quickly away. She sits down and manages immediately to knock over a vase of anemones. She wants his attention. In a loud voice, she apologizes to the waiter for her clumsiness. De Winter rushes to her rescue and leads her to his table, shrewdly remarking that he would have invited her to join him even if she hadn't upset the vase so clumsily. He assures her they needn't talk to each other if they don't feel like it. She demurs. She pretends, especially to herself, that she is awkward, flustered, shy. Certainly not one to stage an encounter.

One of her first comments to Maxim de Winter is about her dead father, a painter who painted the same tree over and over, on the theory that once you have found the perfect thing or place or person, you should stick with it. "Do you think that's very silly?" she asks, and a more seductive, loaded question is hardly imaginable. With what de Winter calls her funny, lost look and her coded language, she is irresistible. Of course she will win the master of the manor for herself.

Women make gestures and then refuse to acknowledge them as if there were a split between our actions and our motives, which we conveniently bury from ourselves. Perhaps it's simply that little in our training has allowed us to acknowledge our manipulation of men.

We were also trained never openly to initiate romantic

episodes. When I was a child we used to sing a rhyme as we skipped rope:

> On the mountain stands a Lady,
> Who she is I do not know.
> All she wants is gold and silver,
> All she wants is a nice young man.

We sang it over and over, its words tracing grooves in our brains. Waiting patiently was imbued with romance.

But there was a hidden animus in that rhyme. Relentlessly waiting, we were also predatory. Greedy for gold and silver. As females we couldn't initiate, but then we were faulted for passivity, which was synonymous with parasitism. No wonder it was so difficult to lay claim to our own actions.

I recall another gesture from a second film, *The Lover*, based on the autobiographical novel by Marguerite Duras. The story records the obsession of a thirty-two-year-old Chinese man for a fifteen-year-old white girl. (She has told him she is seventeen.) The story opens with one of the most delicately evocative scenes in film.

The young girl is taking the ferry across the Mekong River, back to her boarding school in Saigon. She stands on the deck looking at the water. She leans into the railing and lifts one knee, hooking the heel of her shoe on a lower rung. She is wearing a man's fedora, black high-heeled shoes covered with rhinestones, and a low-waisted beige sundress. Her gesture is provocative, sexual, innocent, latent with invitation. Over these images, the eerily disembodied voice of a woman recalls the thrill of rebellion.

The words she speaks are taken directly from Duras' novel and are meant to represent the author's own voice:

> No woman, no girl, wore a man's fedora in that
> colony then. No native woman, either ... the hat, [I]
> am never parted from it. Having got it, this hat that
> all by itself makes me whole, I wear it all the time.

That provocative hat, the object that makes her whole, is the very thing that brands her a little slut in the eyes of the other passengers. Whore/whole. Duras has caught the paradox. By living the innocence of her desire, the potency of her sexuality, by ignoring the world's terms, she begins to recover from the damage of a brutalizing childhood. The man is exquisite, his reverence extreme. For Duras, it is he who is broken by love and she who is healed.

At the age of eighteen, Duras left Vietnam and returned to France, where she wrote her novel and became a famous writer. Nowadays, the relationship she described could never be painted in such sepia tones. She was just a child, fifteen and a half, and what prevents this relationship from being dangerous is, disturbingly, the colonial and class context that dictates that a white girl has power over a mature Chinese man.

A friend of mine tells me that when she was sixteen, she, like Duras, picked up a man. She met him in the basement book section of a large department store in Montreal. He was small, exotic, dashingly French. She wonders whether it is her memory that invents a blue beret. He must have been about thirty. She caught his attention with a seductive smile. He smiled back. She left the store, glancing back, and he followed. She knew nothing of sex, but she felt the hot desire in her body. Before she knew it she was in his apartment, in his bed. Luckily she was menstruating, and when he felt the blood, he informed her that one didn't do this thing they were doing at such times. He treated her like the child she was. But as they left he steered her through the kitchen where two men sat playing poker. To display her? How close had she come to disaster? No young girl could be so ignorant today. But all she was doing was living the imperative of erotic desire that everything in her wanted to experience. Dangerous for a woman.

My point in these stories is to ask whether there is a place for female desire. How do we initiate it? Express it? Do we get to assume control of our own gestures? Are we able, even now, to take an aggressive role in expressing our own sexuality without inviting confusion, contempt, or, worse, violence?

8

The Body

*She watched his fingers, the bones beneath his skin. She wanted
this man.*

Romantic obsession thrives in the body. It must be based
on sex, and sex is the body's best gift. Yet even more
potent is desire.

Our bodies work like filter systems. With our most
sophisticated telescopes, we see only 8 percent of the
cosmic activity in the night sky. The rest escapes us. The
ocean, to us, is the most silent space on the planet. Were
our ears attuned to its decibels, we would hear a cacoph-
ony that would drive us crazy. We survive only because
the body is able to filter out excess. Most often we negotiate our way comfortably, faithfully processing the physical world in ordered ways. More and more, we keep the
world at a distance.

When I talk with my friend Laurie Maher about the
body, she gets desperate. She believes that we have lost

the body. "I think about evolution," she says. "Man evolving: animal, *Homo erectus*, bionic man. Our brain has grown until our body is this little nub hanging off the brain. We walk around hanging off our brains. We need to feel. We need the body back."

We long for the feeling of desire because desire puts us back in our bodies. In the state of desire, the mind dissolves and the body focuses. Think of a cat watching a bird. Its attention is total, its whole body a taut wire humming with one motive only. That's the kind of absolute, intense physical at-tension I mean. That's how we feel when we desire.

As adolescents most of us discovered the body harbored a mystery. Going down, down, down to a place where sensation took over, building to a pitch of such intensity that the body shuddered with its own electricity. The body gathered into one ecstatic center and then, suddenly, there was a flood of release and it became liquid fire. We had discovered the body's magic.

And from that moment we hungered for the body's electric connections. Sex fires the nerve endings. Not much in our world is as intense as this flash point of physical pleasure.

But sex as a physical act is merely athletics, a momentary relief. What it needs to be powerful is desire, and the strongest element of desire is longing. It's in the word. *De sider-, sidus:* from the stars. The longing that reaches beyond space and time.

9

Passion's Chemistry

The world came alive as they sat there. She was aware of the sudden heat of his hand on her arm, his beautiful elongated fingers playing across her knuckles, the mixed odor of wet pavement and caramel and coffee, even a little hummingbird rarely seen in Mexico City—a chuparrosa, he called it— sucking the pink bougainvillea on the wall of the café.

When we fall in love the world wakes up. The chemistry of the whole universe has changed. Even looking back at the times I myself was romantically obsessed, what I most miss is that waking up of the world.

It has to do with the sensation of alignment, of focus, that comes with wanting someone so clearly, so utterly. I remember sitting with my lover on a peninsula of rock jutting out to sea, watching the autumn sun rise. I held his face in my hands. Black seals slipped among the barnacled rocks and gulls threaded the cold air. I had seen this landscape many times before, but suddenly it was utterly altered and fused with longing. Could anything have been more romantic?

In books, as in life, such moments stand out like holograms; three-dimensional, they linger in the mind. There is a passage in Boris Pasternak's *Doctor Zhivago*, undoubtedly one of the great love stories of the twentieth century. The backdrop of the novel is the Russian Revolution, and although everything, even love, is destroyed in its name, the love affair between Zhivago and Lara provides a momentary respite. For years they have encountered and evaded each other, but the obsession proves too powerful. Zhivago is returning to Lara as her lover:

> He is on his way to her. In a moment he will leave the wooden sidewalks and vacant lots for the paved streets. The small suburban houses flash by like the pages of a book. ... over there is her house at the far end of the street, under the white gap in the rain clouds where the sky is clearing, toward the evening. How he loves the little houses in the street that lead to her! He could pick them up and kiss them! Those one-eyed attics with their roofs pulled down like caps. And the lamps and icon lights reflected in the puddles and shining like berries! And her house under the white rift of the sky! ... A dark muffled figure will open the door, and the promise of her nearness, unowned by anyone in the world and guarded and cold as a white northern

light, will reach him like the first wave of the sea as
you run down over the sandy beach in the dark.

As we read, we know that Pasternak has known this
dazzling sense of inflation as even the inanimate world
wakes to his sense of longing.

Many modern biologists claim that nature has set us up
for this mad infatuation. It's not the least bit interested in
our fantasies. It has its own plot, always sending us
towards another with reproduction in mind. Apparently,
when we fall in love, the levels of the neurotransmitters
dopamine, norepinephrine, and phenylethylamine change
in our bodies, creating a powerful cocktail of natural
amphetamines that spark euphoria. It seems nature
reserves its best reward for us when we follow its rules.

Dr. Steven Pinker, professor of cognitive neuroscience
at the Massachusetts Institute of Technology, even
suggests that romantic love may be biologically
programmed. He claims that hundreds of thousands of
years of evolution have hard-wired certain concepts in
the human brain, "including social intelligence (the ability to impute motives and desires to other people), a
sense of justice, and romantic love."

Of course, the only thing this suggests is that such
conditions are real. But why are we programmed for
romantic love? That is the mystery.

10

Models

Perhaps it was the black hair reaching to his shoulders that gave him a kind of seductive arrogance that she found pleasurable to look at. ... How was it possible to feel so immediately intimate with a complete stranger?

It was the Romantic Movement at the end of the eighteenth century that laid down the model of the male lover that we still subscribe to today. He has various names: the bohemian artist, the demon lover, the Byronic hero. The only criteria that define him are that he must be sensitive, he must have that seductive quality of aloofness, and he must suffer.

There once was a man named Goethe. That's how I think of him—as a generic fact, so great was the influence he had on the European imagination. In 1774, at the age of twenty-five, Goethe wrote *The Sorrows of Young Werther*, the confessional story of a young artist who falls passionately in love with a woman already betrothed to another, and when she rejects him, he is driven to commit suicide. The book was immediately seen as autobiographical. It was clearly the story of Goethe's unrequited love for the young Charlotte Buff.

Werther sold fabulously and was soon translated into every European language. Men began to wear Werther's blue frock coat, leather waistcoat, and yellow breeches. Women wore *Werther* jewelry, gloves, and fans, and even Eau de *Werther* cologne. Entrepreneurs marketed *Werther* paraphernalia. Tea sets were painted with scenes from the novel. In Vienna, there was a *Werther* fireworks display.

Pilgrimages were made to the grave where the fictional Werther was supposed to have been buried and to the linden tree where Goethe was said to have liked to sit. A young woman drowned herself in the River Ilm behind Goethe's garden in Weimar with a copy of *Werther* in her pocket. Another jumped from a tower in Munich. When James Hackman murdered Martha Reay outside Covent Garden in 1779 and then tried to shoot himself, the British novelist Sir Herbert Croft worked up the affair into an epistolary novel called *Love and Madness* in which he suggested Hackman had been reading *The Sorrows of Young Werther*. The city council of Leipzig banned *Werther* as encouraging suicide.

There were those who wanted to imitate not the character's suicide but rather the novel's success. *Werther* was made the subject of operas, plays, poems, and songs; hack writers rewrote it with a happy ending.

By then, Goethe was thoroughly fed up. "I am heartily tired of having poor *Werther* exhumed and dissected," he remarked.

But what was the true story behind that book's composition? Goethe had fallen in love with Charlotte Buff, but she was already "intended" for another. After a summer of triangular and decorous love, Goethe left for the city of Koblenz, where he met Maximiliane, the sixteen-year-old daughter of a friend. "It is very pleasant," he wrote later, "if a new passion awakens within us before the old one has quite faded away."

He wrote his novel in four weeks; it was a story of what for him was the best part of romantic love, "the happiness we experience when we desire what we cannot have." He wrote in his autobiography, "If, as they say, the greatest happiness is to be found in longing, and if true longing must always be directed to something unattainable, then everything conspired to make the youth [Goethe liked to refer to himself in the third person] whose fortunes we are following the happiest mortal on earth."

The suicide plot of the book was based on a friend, Karl Jerusalem, who shot himself when rejected by a married woman. "It was loneliness, God knows, that ate away at his heart," Goethe said.

The public read *Werther* as a true love story, but Goethe was bored with it. Being a young author, he was more interested in fame and immortality than in love. (It's almost impossible to credit, but if his biographers are to be trusted, Goethe's first sexual experience occurred in Italy when he was almost forty. After returning to Germany, he met a twenty-three-year-old Weimar workingwoman, Christiane Vulpius, who became his mistress and eventually his wife.)

When he was obsessed as a young man with Charlotte Buff, Goethe didn't really want the woman so much as the feeling of rapturous passion that she occasioned and that gave him his book. Few authors would choose the woman rather than the book. But girls, in particular, kept thinking that Goethe was serious. Even into his old age they hunted him down as the object of their romantic passion. His most famous groupie was Bettina. A young married woman, she would come to sit on Goethe's knee. Obsessively, she wrote him love letters. After his death, she published them, having carefully edited his side of the correspondence so that the passion could be seen to be requited. She was after immortality too—she wanted to be objectified in history as the muse, the most passionate female love object.

The most profound consequence of the novel was the creation of the cult of the male genius exempt from the conventional rules of society, the cult that would lead to Byron and Beethoven. The sentimental, melancholic Werther would become transformed into the virile misanthrope, the proto-Romantic hero. Genius was assigned exclusively to the male and was associated with potency. The result of passion was art. For women, though, passion was the end in itself. The early-nineteenth-century American writer Washington Irving was not atypical in remarking:

> Shall I confess it?—I believe in broken hearts, and the possibility of dying of disappointed love! I do not, however, consider it a malady often fatal to my own sex; but I firmly believe that it withers down many a lovely woman into an early grave. ... Man is the creature of interest and ambition ... but a woman's whole life is a history of the affections.

So many prescriptive myths for women. Now women had to find a man worth dying for.

11

The Demon Lover

He seemed to know everything about Mexican art. He dazzled her with stories of the damas de corazón, about all their scandals and love affairs.

Have you noticed how we live our love affairs as if they were great dramas? Lovers have their own secret locations, their own songs, sometimes even their own films—the first time I fell in love I thought I was reliving *Doctor Zhivago*. And we tell our love stories in ways that demand a suspension of disbelief. They are meant to sound improbable, outrageous, and exotic. No one has ever loved with such intensity. Our passions elevate us into a class with the great love stories in history.

Why do we tell our love stories so compulsively? Why do they have to be spoken? Maybe it's because they are, in part, performances, and they need an audience. Once, in a women's washroom of a local university, I watched a pretty young woman talking in the mirror to her friend. As she adjusted her hair she said petulantly: "None of my friends can figure out why I'm in love with a criminal who's in Kingston Penitentiary." I smiled in the mirror and I could see she was pleased with the effect she'd made. Part of the point of her loving a criminal was the shock effect it had on others. It was dangerous. To love against the world's terms, against the normalizing, the quotidian, was brave. To love as the world is afraid to do conferred status, heroism. I thought, "Ah, yes, the demon lover."

Perhaps La Rochefoucauld was right when he suggested that we pattern our love affairs after literary models. Certainly, the demon lover has been part of our collective imagination for centuries. Yet nowhere did he find a more impressive home than in the novels of two nineteenth-century sisters. When Emily and Charlotte Brontë published their novels in 1847, I wonder whether they had any idea what they were unleashing on the cultures of the future: countless women looking for their own Rochesters and Heathcliffs.

How do some characters become so powerful that they walk out of the pages of a book and take up residence in the real world? It's probably because, like all mythological beings, they touch us at the level of our deepest fears and longings.

The story of *Wuthering Heights* is familiar. A kindly preacher brings to his home on the moors a city urchin he found abandoned in the streets of Liverpool. Uncouth and uneducated, the child attaches himself to the young daughter of the family, and she returns his devotion. Cathy and Heathcliff become vagabonds running wild on the moors. But at sixteen, Cathy marries a neighbor, a man of wealth and position. Betrayed, Heathcliff flees, mysteriously educates himself, becomes a wealthy gentleman, returns, and spends the rest of his life as a misanthrope seeking revenge for his unhappiness.

It doesn't sound promising, but in Emily Brontë's hands, the story takes on mythic proportions: the brooding lovers on the brooding moors. The most famous passage in the novel is Cathy's explanation to her nurse of why she loves Heathcliff:

> Whatever our souls are made of, his and mine are the same. ... surely you and everybody have a notion that there is, or should be an existence of yours beyond you. What were the use of my creation if I were entirely contained here? ... If all else perished, and *he* remained, I should still continue to be; and, if all else remained, and he were annihilated, the Universe would turn to a mighty stranger. I should not seem a part of it. My love for Linton is like the foliage in the woods. Time will change it, I'm well aware, as winter changes the trees—my love for Heathcliff resembles the eternal rocks beneath—a source of little visible delight, but necessary. Nelly, I *am* Heathcliff.

But who is Heathcliff? He is a man who brutalizes the world and yet is preternaturally faithful to one woman. In the real world, a man capable of marrying his beloved's sister-in-law out of contempt, strangling his wife's pet dog for pleasure, and intentionally demeaning a child out of revenge would also be abusive towards his lover. But Heathcliff is a female fantasy, the counterpart to a male fantasy: the whore with the heart of gold. He is a narcissistic man who treats life as if it owes him, violently takes what he wants, and yet is honorable at the core. Even if Heathcliff *were* a psychological possibility, he wouldn't be good company.

Critics have noted that it was a clergyman's daughter who created this archetype of the male, monstrous in the intensity and fidelity of his love. Emily Brontë was a twenty-nine-year-old virgin brought up in the isolation of the Yorkshire moors and certainly had no sexual experience of men when she wrote her book. But she did know male violence. Her beloved brother, Branwell, had been driven to the edge of insanity by what the Brontë family considered the unconscionable behavior of his employer, a forty-seven-year-old married woman, Lydia Robinson. Seventeen years his senior, she had coldly seduced him and then dropped him when the affair became inconvenient. Addicted to drugs, Branwell died at the age of thirty-one.

The point, though, is that Emily Brontë's love story has little to do with love in the world. She did not find the models for her lovers in real life. *Wuthering Heights* is about rebelling against limits placed on the spirit by time and by death. It's about secret dreams, dark follies, outlawed love, emotions as pure and elemental as lightning storms, about desiring the instant of passion above any illusion of the future, and about preferring death to life. It's a great mistake to look for Heathcliff in the world.

And what about Rochester, her sister's male archetype, a more domesticated demon lover? I think of Charlotte Brontë making a decision to rewrite female history. She'd read Lord Byron, Goethe, and all those male writers who presented themselves as great lovers in thinly disguised poetic autobiographies. In the mid-1840s, she would do the unheard of and write a book with a *female* protagonist who had her own heroic adventures. In those days, there was only one plot for a woman to write: the love plot. After all, what did Charlotte know of war and voyages? So she invented Jane Eyre.

Jane is orphaned and penniless—no parents to tell her what to do. Her plot is simple: how to win a modicum of freedom in a world run on money and male power. The solution will have to be marriage, but the dilemma is whether to marry the clergyman or the demon lover. Of course she chooses the demon lover. The little governess will tame and win the Master, a brooding and possibly dangerous man.

What makes this goal possible is that Rochester has a secret that causes him great suffering. Jane will have to save him again and again. (So many women still hold on to fantasies of saving men.) When Rochester falls off his horse the very first time they meet, Jane helps him up. When his bed catches fire, she wakes him and puts out the fire. He treats her with contempt, teases her with his flirtations with beautiful society ladies, and all the while she, plain Jane, sews quietly in the corner and looks after his illegitimate daughter. It's all really to test her mettle.

Rochester's secret, as everyone knows, is his mad wife in the attic. However, this doesn't reflect badly on him. It was his father's fault. Being the penniless second son, he'd been married off for money, just as if he were a helpless female. He's forgiven for everything: the illegitimate child, the bigamous proposal to Jane, even the imprisonment of his wife. (In Victorian times rich people commonly hid their mad relations in attics.) When his wife sets fire to the mansion, he tries to save her. Mutilated and badly burned, he is finally needy enough for Jane. She wins him by her moral superiority, with a dollop of coquetry on the side. It's an appalling ending: Rochester, blind and maimed, led around the garden by the intrepid Jane. She has made herself indispensable. Is this the best Jane Eyre can do? Probably. Rochester comes with an estate.

Unlike her sister Emily, Charlotte Brontë had had some erotic experience by the time she wrote *Jane Eyre*. She'd been to Belgium and fallen into a platonic love affair with a married man. By her mid-twenties, she had tasted the humiliations of the role of governess, having been employed by a *nouveau riche* family of merchants. For her, the worst part of the job had been the mandatory evenings on display in the drawing room as an accoutrement of their wealth. Lonely, and hating her enforced subservience, she knew she was wasting her talents. She conceived the plan of opening a school for young ladies with her sisters, and to her surprise her aunt Branwell offered to finance their efforts.

But first, a formal and continental education was required. Half a year at a foreign school to perfect their French and German, with perhaps a little Italian, would be just the thing to attract pupils from the upper-middle class. In 1842, Charlotte and Emily set out for the Pensionnat Heger in Brussels, a "Maison d'Education pour les Jeunes Demoiselles" under the direction of Madame Heger. Charlotte was twenty-six and Emily twenty-four. At first it seemed they'd made a terrible mistake. The oldest pupils in the school, they immediately found themselves isolated among Catholic girls from financially secure, if not wealthy, families; girls who were destined for marriage, and to whom learning was a matter of indifference.

But Charlotte, at least, found a consolation. Constantin Heger, a professor of French and mathematics at a boys' academy, gave lessons in literature at his wife's school, which was also the family residence. By all reports a brilliant teacher, he recognized the accomplishment, indeed originality, of both sisters and took them under his wing. He must have been delighted to find such talented female pupils.

Elizabeth Gaskell, who published a biography of Charlotte two years after her death in 1855, managed to speak with Heger. Of Emily, he remarked that it was a tragedy she was so limited by her sex and poverty: "She should have been a man, a great navigator. Her powerful reason would have deduced new spheres of discovery ... and her strong, imperious will would never have been daunted by opposition." About Charlotte, he was much more circumspect. He had reason to be.

When Emily returned home to England at the end of their course of study, Charlotte elected to stay on and teach at the Pensionnat Heger. At first she was welcomed warmly and treated like a member of the family. Monsieur lent her books and conversed with her, and soon she was giving him and his brother-in-law English lessons. But then Mme. Heger recognized what her husband did not. Charlotte had fallen in love with the Master.

Soon Heger was too busy to give Charlotte lessons in French literature or to continue his own English lessons. At the end of what had become an agonizing year, Charlotte left the school. She wrote to her friend Ellen Nussey: "I suffered much before I left Brussels. I think, however long I live, I shall not forget what the parting with M. Heger cost me; it grieved me so much to grieve him, who has been so true, kind, and disinterested a friend."

Back in England, all Charlotte's endeavors to put their training to good use failed. The Misses Brontë's Establishment for Young Ladies never materialized. Not a single student replied to their advertisement.

Charlotte wrote on a number of occasions to Monsieur, opening her heart just a little. Appalled, he wrote back with the rebuke that he was interested only in her studies and in future she must write infrequently and with restraint. Her correspondence is heartbreaking in its desperation. In her final letter she wrote:

Monsieur,—The six months of silence have run their course. It is now the 18th of Novr.; my last letter was dated (I think) the 18th of May [1846]. I may therefore write to you without failing in my promise. ...

I tell you frankly that I have tried meanwhile to forget you, for the remembrance of a person whom one thinks never to see again, and whom, nevertheless, one greatly esteems, frets too much the mind; and when one has suffered that kind of anxiety for a year or two, one is ready to do anything to find peace once more. I have done everything; I have sought occupations; I have denied myself absolutely the pleasure of speaking about you—even to Emily; but I have been able to conquer neither my regrets nor my impatience. That, indeed, is humiliating—to be unable to control one's own thoughts, to be the slave of a regret, of a memory, the slave of a fixed and dominant idea which lords it over the mind. Why cannot I have just as much friendship for you, as you for me—neither more nor less? Then should I be so tranquil, so free—I could keep silence then for ten years without an effort. ...

To forbid me to write to you, to refuse to answer me would be to tear from me my only joy on earth, to deprive me of my last privilege—a privilege I shall never consent willingly to surrender. Believe me, my master, in writing to me it is a good thing that you will do. So long as I believe you are pleased with me, so long as I have hope of receiving news from you, I can be at rest and not too sad. But when a prolonged and gloomy silence seems to threaten me with estrangement of my master—when day by day I await a letter, and when day by day disappointment comes to fling me back into overwhelming sorrow, and the sweet delight of seeing your handwriting and reading your counsel escapes me as a vision that is vain, then fever claims me—I lose appetite and sleep—I pine away.

May I write to you again next May? I would rather wait a year, but it is impossible—it is too long.

C. Brontë

Charlotte never heard from her Master again.
The ardor in this letter is uncanny. M. Heger is fiction,

a phantom onto whom she had hooked all her needs. All that feeling so badly misplaced.

No biographer of Charlotte Brontë has ever suggested impropriety on the part of Constantin Heger. Yet as a teacher, he seduced her unwittingly with his mind and his love of literature. It must have been flattering to have a young woman as devoted and intelligent as Charlotte Brontë to mold intellectually. When he finally recognized the firestorm he had created, and abruptly stopped their correspondence, he surely must have felt some guilt.

But posterity was the luckier for M. Heger's delicacy. Charlotte's feelings of rage, repression, frustration, longing, and love, which could hardly have been met by this schoolmaster from Brussels, went into the creation of her novel *Villette* and later of her masterpiece *Jane Eyre*.

There are numerous moments when Charlotte's own voice shatters the fictional surface of her novel. My favorite is when Jane is walking on the ramparts of Rochester's mansion and she thinks:

Women are supposed to be very calm generally: but women feel just as men feel; they need exercise for their faculties, and a field for their efforts as much as their brothers do; they suffer from too rigid a restraint, too absolute a stagnation, precisely as men would suffer; and it is narrow-minded in their more privileged fellow-creatures to say that they ought to confine themselves to making puddings and knitting stockings, to playing on the piano and embroidering bags. It is thoughtless to condemn them, or laugh at them, if they seek to do more or learn more than custom has pronounced necessary for their sex.

Suddenly Jane hears insane, demonic laughter. Though she does not know it, the laughter belongs to Rochester's mad wife imprisoned in the attic just a few feet away from where she walks.

This moment always unnerves me, as it did Virginia Woolf, who refers to it in her book *A Room of One's Own*. For me, it's as if Charlotte Brontë is unconsciously asserting that beneath the prim governess is the raging unfulfilled woman who will exact her revenge. As is suggested by her letters from Brussels, Charlotte must often have felt close to insanity trying to deal with her unrequited love. How absurd that a woman of Charlotte Brontë's genius should have had to beg for crumbs of attention at Heger's table.

Still, she got her own back. If she didn't get the man, she got to write the book. She got to one-up her male contemporaries. William Wordsworth and Robert Southey had told her it was unfeminine to write books. More than most of them, she got the kind of fame that lasts over centuries. In real life she married the worthy clergyman, not the Master, and died giving birth to her first child.

It took novelist Jean Rhys to strip the demon lover of his

eternal pretensions. A hundred years after Charlotte
Brontë, she rewrote *Jane Eyre* from the perspective of the
mad wife in the attic. For Charlotte Brontë, Rochester's
first wife, Bertha Mason, was simply a piece of the machin-
ery that drove the plot—the dark secret in Rochester's
past. She had invented a Caribbean background for Bertha
because making her a Creole was safe. She was the exotic
Other, easily demonized, and Victorian readers did not
have to think about her as a real person.

But for Jean Rhys, herself a Creole from the Caribbean,
the Other has a name and is real. These women were
being colonized, and she knew all about that. Born Gwen
Rees Williams in Roseau, Dominica, in 1890, at the age
of seventeen Jean Rhys was sent to England to attend the
Perse High School for Girls, in Cambridge. It was a strict
and spartan Edwardian school, and she stood out as an
exotic. The other girls called her "West Indies." After
graduating, she enrolled in the London Academy of
Dramatic Art, but when her father died suddenly, she was
ordered back home. Refusing to return, she got herself a
job in the chorus of a musical comedy and was soon tour-
ing repertory theaters in the north of England.

The life of a chorus girl was tough (all those cheap
hotels in cold northern towns) but it suited her. Humor-
ous and reckless, she picked up admirers and dropped
them. While working at the Old Lyceum Theatre in
London in a production of *Cinderella* (staged with a glass
coach and real ponies), she met a rich banker's son with

the unlikely name of Lancelot Hugh Smith. Soon she was being kept by Lancelot. After two years the affair ended badly.

Jean Rhys married three times, rather disastrously; two of her three husbands were arrested for fraud and petty crimes. She published four novels and a collection of stories, and then, for twenty-six years, the literary world saw almost nothing of her. She spent those years living in dire poverty; as she said in a letter to an old friend, she was almost always "two days drunk, one day hung over." Then, in her seventy-sixth year, she finally completed the novel she had been mulling over for decades: *Wide Sargasso Sea*. It was her masterpiece.

Unlike the Brontë sisters when they wrote their novels, Jean Rhys knew all about real sex. She knew that sex is dangerous, which may be why we sanitize it with safe, careful words like *intercourse* (from the Latin *inter* and *currere*—running between). Antoinette Mason, the girl whose name Rochester changes to Bertha as he drives her mad, falls for the handsome Englishman and enters the territory of sexual longing. Once Antoinette loves Rochester, she knows he can break her. She is lost and drowned in the power of sex. Desire and hatred come close in the dark.

Why does he break her? Because he can, and because he is afraid of her eroticism; afraid of losing himself to passion; afraid of losing control. "I was thirsty for her," he tells himself, "but that is not love." She is too alien, too disturbing, too secret. And he, the cool-headed English-man, having learned always to hide his innermost feel-ings, pulls back. He will not make himself vulnerable to a woman by showing his need for her. Yet he vows to keep his hold on her. She is *his* lunatic. He takes her money and keeps the key to the attic.

Jean Rhys repeats this one story in all her novels. Waif-like women are impregnated, abandoned, used up, made insane by men. Serial desertion. She once said to her friend the novelist David Plante, "A man needs a woman, but a woman without a man is nothing, nothing." A devastating statement, though perhaps a product of the propaganda of the time. Jean Rhys seemed to believe in such passivity, as if nothing could ever be done. Trapped, forever stuck, a woman could only rage.

Francis Wyndham, a friend of ten years and editor of her letters, wrote that Jean Rhys always had "a feeling of belonging nowhere, of being ill at ease and out of place in her surroundings wherever these happened to be, a stranger in an indifferent, even hostile, world." But this alienation was not simply a product of her exile from the West Indies. Wyndham suggests she was broken by her disastrous first love affair with Lancelot Hugh Smith. Some claimed the affair ended in an "illegal operation."

In one of her notebooks, Jean Rhys quoted the title of the popular song "I'm Going to Lock My Heart and Throw Away the Key." To Wyndham, the phrase suggested "the complex emotional amputation which

Jean performed on herself to prevent any recurrence of the grief and hurt which had overwhelmed her then."

Jean Rhys became one of those casualties of love, an adept at the broken heart. And writing seemed not to have been enough of a consolation. David Plante recalls her saying: "I wonder if it was right to give up so much of my life for writing. I don't think, after all, that my writing was worth it." But then she would contradict herself and say: "Only writing is important. Only writing takes you out of yourself."

12

The First Conversation

And then, unexpectedly, as if he was surprised by his own candor, he began to talk of his life. It was as though he was opening a suitcase, taking out a memory here, an anecdote there, and laying them carefully on the table.

There seems to be a certain point at which it becomes impossible for women to understand how men think, and vice versa. Virginia Woolf used to say that all people are androgynous except for one pin-sized spot at the back of the head where a woman completely differs from a man. One of the good offices each sex provides the other is in describing that blind spot. Women can't fully know who they are unless men tell them; men cannot know themselves fully without the assistance of women.

Women often say that love begins with the first conversation. The actress Annette Bening, referring to her first meeting with Warren Beatty, described this ingenuously: "You're saying everything and they're saying everything, and you're talking about things in a way that makes you feel honest and good." We all long for that moment of intimacy when the lover not only listens but echoes; not only mirrors but enlarges. In that first conversation, facets of ourselves are heard or seen as if for the first time. Something we hadn't put in place or owned is suddenly acknowledged.

For a woman, complete candor on the part of a man is erotic. For most of us, men often seem to live undercover lives, hiding or dissembling their feelings. Men will often say they mistrust intimate conversations. They're invasive, a kind of probing into their brains. Women will say that, when falling in love, men suddenly open up, and are able to be vulnerable.

But there are warnings to be heeded by both sexes here. Sometimes something else entirely is going on.

The fact is, a man will often unconsciously seduce a woman with the narrative of his own loneliness. And a young woman often misconstrues these confessions as an expression of sensitivity. His willingness to tell her of his loneliness is a gift. She feels unique in her capacity to understand him.

The story of the married man and his young mistress is the archetypal model. Unlike his wife, who might translate what he says into self-pity, the young woman hears the husband's suffering and she believes that she alone understands him. She is confident that love is always benevolent. She truly believes that her role as the inter-loper into this marriage is innocent. The unhappy wife would be better off alone. At the beginning, it doesn't occur to her that she herself is a digression; that he prob-ably has a perfectly good wife; that more often than not financial entanglements or children or habit will keep the married couple together; that, in fact, her precise function as the lover is to keep the marriage going. During all those ecstatic rushed secret assignations, she believes she is doing no harm to anyone, least of all herself. She does not know that, given the odds, she is an old story, just a young bit-on-the-side too quickly loved and too easily betrayed.

The idea that love, no matter what damage it causes, is a transcendent good is almost an unwritten axiom of our culture. For this reason, women can be ruthless when they fall obsessively in love. A New York friend of mine woke one day to find that his wife had left him. He was shocked. He believed there had been no clues, though in retrospect he had to admit he had had suspicions and a growing sense of unease. She had fallen in love with a German yachtsman and wanted to live with him. She also wanted custody of their young son, and so she accused my friend of spousal abuse, though she knew this was false. There had been a midnight emergency call to the police on an unrelated matter. The police hadn't come, but the call was logged, and that would provide the evidence. Suddenly my friend was living a nightmare.

What he didn't know was that he was confronting the

revenge of the unlived life. His wife had spent years living his version of their life. When a lover came to offer her the adventure she longed for, she jumped ship. (It's hard not to be amused by the cliché she chose. As in a bad film, with her yachtsman she could sail into the sunset.) But in her mind, erotic love justified her ruthlessness and her angry pursuit of vengeance.

Returning for a moment to the intimacy of that first conversation, I would offer men a warning. Men must not think that all they need to do is open up and be vulnerable to get the woman of their dreams. Often, the intimacy women are falling for, the confessions of vulnerability they seek, are paradoxical. They must be perceived to be offered from strength—*he is strong enough to be vulnerable*.

I think of another friend, a young Greek, so beautiful that I'm sure his genes go back to the boys who posed for those classical statues we revere. His relationships with women always end in disaster. His beauty draws them to him, and then he offers them his need. He asks them to carry the load of his self-doubt, his sense of inadequacy, his entire repertoire of insecurity. Sadly for him, that's never what they had in mind. What's important to a woman about that first conversation is not that the man is confessing but that he is confessing to her alone. A woman doesn't fall in love with a man's need. She falls in love with his need for her.

13

This Gnawing Hunger

But the walls were covered with his paintings. They all had the same title: The Itinerary of a Naked I. *Each painting depicted a figure—sometimes male, sometimes female—standing in a corner, shoulders hunched, about to walk into an empty landscape. Some were red, others blue, green, yellow. The monotony was overwhelming, as if they were stuck. She felt that in the recesses of his mind she was looking into the mirror of her own loneliness.*

When I was ten, I cut my face from many of the family photographs. When I look at them now, there is a small hole sitting in the corner. I remember my mother was angry at the defacement of the family heirlooms. I wonder now whether to her it was a simple act of mischief, or did she realize that this child was trying so diligently to abdicate from the family? I cannot recover the moment. I do not remember myself as a timid or angry child, though I was certainly shy. When I reconstruct the act, it is being carried out with resilience and a fierce attention. I believe I was removing myself from the scene. I was learning to use a strategy of silently disappearing in order to negotiate my own way. Of course that kind of fierce will has an enormous price. It took years to break from the circumscribed exclusion I had invented for myself. And for years I carried that hole in the small of my back. I could feel it, quite literally, in moments of intense emotion. Much later, when I read that anorexic girls had that same sensation of having holes, but in their stomachs, I knew exactly what they meant. I had constructed a defensive carapace around myself. It covered me completely, except for that small hole.

A poet friend once told me of a dream she'd had. She was kneeling beside a mermaid whose back was covered with fine green grass. My friend's task was to pluck the grass, blade by blade. She was horrified because she knew that what lay under that grass was that same gaping hole. What is this gnawing hunger? The first time I fell in love, I asked my lover to cover that spot with his hand, make the hole disappear.

Perhaps all romantic love is the search for a defense against emptiness. And perhaps the more desperate the search, the more obsessive the love.

In "Autumn Day," Rainer Maria Rilke writes:

> Whoever has no house now will never build one.
> Whoever is alone will stay alone a long time,
> Will lie awake, read, write long letters through the
>   night,
> Or wander aimlessly in alleys, as the leaves stir ...

A cell cannot survive alone. Unless other cells signal it to stay alive, it will die. To fear being alone is natural. We need intimates, not least to help us discover ourselves. But some of us are more needy than others. Some of us picked up the habit of loneliness in childhood when we learned what we could and could not expect to deserve from the world.

There is also a metaphysical aspect to our loneliness. Human consciousness comes at a cost. At birth we fall from undifferentiated bliss into our solitary identities. Every culture has a story of a fall from paradise. But though we may fall *from* paradise, we fall *into* love. It's love that brings us, if only briefly, a sense of being not separate, of being matched, mirrored, met. It is a returning to what life should have been.

Someone once said that sex, not religion, is the heart in a heartless world. Sex promises warmth and intimacy, and the pleasurable flesh. But beware. It also holds the risk of pain. We negotiate our fears and needs through sex. Often we negotiate our self-worth as well.

The mirroring effects of love allow us to see ourselves as our lovers see us. We fall in love with our lover's version of us. We are the one most beloved and gorgeous creature in the world. Heady stuff. And when love dissolves, we are sent reeling. We no longer amaze and enthrall ourselves, and it breaks our hearts.

14

Sex and Desire

She felt he was peeling back her skin layer by layer with his tongue. And the way he spread her legs before entering her made it a ceremony. Her legs trembled like stalks in wind as she came again and again. She was as high as she'd ever been.

"You're so good at this," he laughed.

How is sex different for a man and for a woman? One enters and the other is entered. Entering implies mastery and control. Being entered demands trust. Having a penis inside is an invasion. Of course, one can love this pleasurable invasion, since it also requires mastery to make the instrument rise.

But when a woman falls in love with (as opposed to has sex with) a man who tells her "You are good at this," it comes as a jolt. *This*, for her, is not a separate act. For this man, sex is consummately a physical thing. While she is busy offering herself up like a virgin, he's preoccupied with performance.

The novelist Bonnie Burnard writes in *A Good House*:

A man's physical attention, occasional or otherwise, should not be taken as hard evidence of anything. That wondrous, breakneck need that appeared to speak for something too complex for words, something beyond ordinary articulation and astonishing and touching in even the most mundane men, spoke for nothing but itself.

That need, the climax. Can a woman possibly know what a man feels? Whatever it is, a man must always achieve it. Anything else is construed by both sexes as failure, either on his part or on hers. Orgasm happens or it doesn't for women, and when it doesn't, women rarely consider it failure. The intimacy is usually enough.

I wonder about women and sex. What brings the most satisfaction?

I carry in my memory a statue I once saw in the Jardin de Luxembourg in Paris. A nymph lay in the arms of her lover while water cascaded over them from a fountain above. I was mesmerized by the smile on her face. It was a smile of complete surrender to desire. I hadn't ever seen that in a sculpture—total erotic satisfaction on a woman's face.

Of course men fall in love too. And that must also involve an act of surrender. It can occur only in a space, beyond self-consciousness or performance, where there is total trust. Alice Munro describes it this way:

> On the bed a woman lies in a yellow nightgown which has not been torn but has been pulled off her shoulders and twisted up around her waist so that it covers no more of her than a crumpled scarf would. A man bends over her, naked, offering a drink of water. The woman, who has almost lost consciousness, whose legs are open, arms flung out, head twisted to the side as if she has been struck down in the course of some natural disaster—this woman rouses herself and tries to hold the glass in her shaky hands. She slops water over her breast, drinks, shudders, falls back. The man's hands are trembling, too. He drinks out of the same glass, looks at her, and laughs. His laugh is rueful, apologetic, and kind, but it is also amazed, and his amazement is not far from horror. How are we capable of all this? his laugh says, what is the meaning of it?
>
> He says, "We almost finished each other off." ...
>
> The room is brimming with gratitude and pleasure, a rich broth of love, a golden twilight of love. Yes, yes, you can drink the air.

It's hard to remember that sexuality is a construct, that the idea of the body changes. Before the middle of the eighteenth century (the century variously called the Age of Enlightenment and the Age of Reason), it was believed that male and female bodies were essentially the same, though the female was less perfect. According to the literary historian Thomas Laqueur in his book *Making Sex*, Galen, the second-century Greek physician and writer on medicine, had developed a powerful model of the human body that demonstrated that male and female reproductive organs were identical: "women were essentially men in whom a lack of vital heat—of perfection—had resulted in the retention, inside, of the structures that in the male are visible without." The externalized sexual organs of the male could all be found in the female, but inside: the vagina was an interior penis, the labia was a foreskin, the uterus a scrotum, and the ovaries were testicles. (In fact the ovaries were called by the same name as male testicles.)

You can see where this is leading. If men ejaculated seed, so did women. If men needed orgasm to come, so too did women. Women might have been seen as less perfect, but if a man wanted progeny, he had better learn how to please his wife.

Galen was translated into Latin during the eleventh and twelfth centuries, and his writings dominated the development of medieval medicine. Laqueur explains that almost every manual on midwifery or marriage (and these existed in all the European languages) "reported it as a commonplace that 'when the seed issues in the act of generation [from both men and women] there at the same time arises an extra-ordinary titillation and delight in all the members of the body.'" The manuals, of necessity, included advice on how to sexually stimulate women to come to orgasm, since without orgasm women could not conceive.

But the Age of Enlightenment made the discovery that the sexes were opposites. Women were alien creatures, intrinsically different from men. This was not a consequence of new medical knowledge. "Sometime in the eighteenth century," Laqueur writes, "sex as we know it was invented." The context was political. In the Age of Reason, it was no longer reasonable to argue that women were inferior because they were a lower form of nature. A new rationalization for the power relationship between the sexes had to be found. Women's bodies became the arena of control: "Women owe their manner of being to their organs of generation, and especially to the uterus," as the eighteenth-century physician C.M. Gardien put it. The orgasm needed for ejaculation and, therefore, for reproduction became an exclusively male phenomenon.

In this way, the rights of women to sexual pleasure were slowly eroded until all forms of female eroticism began to be viewed with deep suspicion. By the end of the eighteenth century it was believed that most women didn't have sexual feelings. By the Victorian era, decent women showed no signs of erotic response. They were to lie back submissively, open their legs, and, as Lady Hillingham famously put it, think of England.

Promiscuity in a woman was even considered grounds

for insanity. It was all very hypocritical. Syphilitic husbands slept with prostitutes while their wives maintained their virtue. Some Victorian gentlemen kept their whips and leather hidden away in drawers.

There are reasons for modern women to regret the Age of Enlightenment.

15

Dreams

That night she dreamed she was walking in labyrinths,
entering caves, finding hidden crypts. In the dream Varian
offered her a sardine can filled with penises and asked her to
choose one.
    She awoke suddenly. All her boundaries were giving way.

Opening to another is risky business. When we fall in
love, the psyche wakes up. Love is dangerous. Sometimes
it even feels like a calamity.

When we're in love, the dreams we wake from can be
full of information. Somehow the admonition in those
dreams is to know ourselves, but what is it we need to
know?

It was a poet, Gwendolyn MacEwen, who told me her
dream about penises. The dream was so absurd I have
never forgotten it. Her lover was seducing her with his
little can of fish. Was he warning her that he had many

spare penises for other women? Or was he assuring her that he had many others where that one came from? And why, in her mind, would penises be squeezed into a can like sardines?

I've always believed that certain dreams are encoded riddles to be solved. In this dream, all the dreamer is sure of is that she is afraid. She has to discover where the problem lies. Is it her own mistrust, or has she already intuited that this man will prove a slippery catch?

In his fascinating book *Private Myths: Dreams and Dreaming*, psychiatrist and neurologist Anthony Stevens contends that our thought processes continue in sleep. Dreams are simply another, more archaic form of thinking. In fact, they are brain experiments. Those skills necessary for survival during the day are rehearsed by the mind at night.

Such theories of dreaming derive from the study of animals. By incapacitating the nerve centers that inhibit movement in sleep, researchers have been able to study sleeping animals as they act out their dreams: cats stalk, pounce on, kill, and eat hallucinatory prey; dogs dig for bones; the hunted flee from their phantom hunters.

Biologically, dreams are a pre-human survival mechanism and come from that part of the mammalian brain that releases the dopamine neurons, stimulating the mind's seeking system, its wanting system, its motivational system—in short, its wishing system.

The question then is, What necessary skills are we

humans rehearsing in dreams? What wishes are we re-enacting?

My first great passion was for a married man, when I was still too young to know better. I had a dream that I can still recall in vivid detail. I was standing on the porch of my childhood home (that porch had been torn down when I was ten years old), and a young woman I knew brought me a large box wrapped in beautiful silk. As I looked down the street, the telephone wires were hung with yellow banners. A Roman wall lined with military statues bisected the street. The wall suddenly caught fire and all the statues jumped from their niches. A voice shouted: "La loi romaine, c'est finie" (the Roman law is finished).

At the time, the dream signified to me the great love affair I was having. I could only see, in those yellow banners, the allusion to *The Song of Solomon*: "His banner over me was love." It wasn't until years later that I understood that my dreaming mind intuited, long before I did, my true situation.

I did not see that the young woman who'd brought the beautiful gift was doing so from complicated motives. She herself was hopelessly in love with this man. In my dream she offered him to me as a gift, knowing that our love affair would shatter his marriage and that I would always be identified with the guilt he felt for this. She was right. He did leave his wife, but not for me. He and the young woman eventually married.

I couldn't have known then that in the end this wouldn't matter to me. Indeed, a sustained relationship with this man would have proved a disaster. But he helped me break the rigid law of conformity (the Roman law) that was the legacy of my Catholic childhood and that had held me in a vise. He did indeed prove a gift, but not in the way I would have anticipated.

I believe in what I call the interior calendar. By this I mean that the deep mind moves at its own pace and the conscious mind, like an obedient child, follows it. That deep part of my mind had already read the landscape. It then leaned back indulgently and watched the sentimental plot unfold. It even made fun of me—those statues leaping in panic from the Roman wall. (At the time, I recognized the wall as the backdrop to the Roman amphitheater in the city of Orange in Provence, which I had recently visited. Not even the Forum is a more impressive symbol of Roman imperialism.) How ready our conscious minds are to deceive us, to hold on to our illusions. If we are paying attention, though, there is a wiser part that sees, that knows.

For better or worse, obsessive love awakens the whole range of primitive emotions of the needy self and we find ourselves caught in a world of mirrors, looking in astonishment at the multiple selves that occupy our inner world. And we thought we knew ourselves! But the feeling of losing control, of our boundaries giving way, is the first step in an important initiation. Obsessive love sends us deep inside the caverns of our own psyches, where, if we have the stamina, we will discover how rich, how resonant, how numinous we are.

16

Tantalus Love

"My mother was disappointed in America. She always longed
for the old days in France. My arrival was an accident. She
stopped painting, and it was my fault. Eventually she stopped
doing anything. You can spend a lifetime making up for stuff
like that."

She was disconcerted by the knife-edge of bitterness in his
voice, yet she was moved by the depth of his hurt. She wanted
to soothe him, to tell him that not everyone betrayed.

When we are in the throes of romantic obsession, it's
intriguing how easily we take the lover's word for it,
putting a positive spin on negative traits. We idealize. If
we didn't, it wouldn't be obsessive love. As he maligns his
mother/father/brother, etc., speaking of the unresolved
hurts of childhood, we marvel at the world from his point
of view. Of course, this may be our own point of view

too. Underneath the compost of us all is childish hurt and anger. As a friend of mine put it, we carry the family wars within us. But why does love bring out those hurts? Perhaps because love offers a physical intimacy that we have not known since childhood. Physically and emotionally naked in the arms of a lover, we feel, at least momentarily, totally safe.

The danger for the woman in my story is that she is becoming absorbed in the man's pain. He goes on and on about himself, and she has not noticed that he neither requires nor expects any contribution from her. I mean her to mistake his solipsism for sensitivity.

I suppose I'm thinking about how often we assume we *know* the other person and how stubborn we can be in our self-delusion.

In 1980, I fled to London after the disintegration of my first love affair. It was late fall. London was bleak and foggy. Everywhere billboards and subway ads were selling products with images of elegant couples in close embrace. I had never felt so alone, or so angry at the world for peddling love. The name of the writer Elizabeth Smart surfaced in the London papers, for she had brought out a new book after a silence of thirty-three years. Her first novel, *By Grand Central Station I Sat Down and Wept*, published in 1945, was already a classic. Its plot was the story I was living: a young woman falls in love with a married man. The lovers flee across America, but then, torn between the two women, he returns to his wife. The young woman is left waiting in a coffee shop in Grand Central Station.

The novel is the generic story of romantic obsession, of falling madly in love and then losing the gamble, but written with such sensuality, such metaphoric intensity that it is utterly seductive. I had an impulse to know how the author had survived her book. It had been so real to me that I presumed she must have lived out its story of romantic disaster.

Though she had been living in England since 1943, Elizabeth Smart was born in Canada. I wrote to her from London as a fellow Canadian, and she invited me to her cottage, the Dell, in Suffolk. It was winter, and I can still remember how desolate the cottage looked, huddled beside a vast empty gravel pit. The landscape was strewn with frozen pools of standing water interrupted by cranes rising like pterodactyls. Elizabeth stood at the gate waiting for me, disheveled in mackinaw and gum boots. She was sixty-five. Her face was lined and lived in, yet somehow as young as a child's. Everything about her was ingenuous, particularly her shyness. I felt like an interloper into her intense privacy. She struck me as incredibly lonely. Years later, though, I would discover that her house was open to everyone, like Grand Central Station itself—the taxi driver was invited in with the passenger.

Inside, the cottage rambled hodgepodge fashion, comfortable in all its discomfort as only an English cottage can be. It felt like the home of a woman used to living alone. I particularly remember the kitchen, which centered on a pulsing coal fire. The moped her children had bought her at sixty sat on the stone floor (she had been stranded for days because its narrow wheels could not negotiate through the snow). The curtains were William Morris prints, and there were books everywhere. A portrait of herself dominated the sitting room: a young woman, wildly beautiful, looking like the French lieutenant's woman with hair blowing as stiff as sails against a rocky landscape, the gaze full of romantic challenge. Looking at it, she appeared amused and bemused by the irony of life's ability to deflate us.

Over an exquisite meal of sole *bonne femme*, we talked of Canada, of lovers, of writing. I asked about her novel and why the man with whom the narrator was so desperately in love was a shadow, almost faceless.

"Of course he has no face," she replied impatiently. "He's a love object."

We had had too much to drink and decided we should rest if we were to make anything of the evening. Elizabeth led me upstairs to the spare room. I climbed into the high four-poster under layers of blankets clutching the hot water bottle she'd given me. When I woke my head was still spinning. I could hear Elizabeth in the next room flailing in her sleep, and crying eerily: "Mother, Mother." The intense longing in that cry was unnerving. It filled the whole house. She was still a stranger to me and I was too shy to mention what I'd heard. Years later I read in her journal: "I am 63. I still scream, cry out at night; heard throughout the house, through several walls, still wrestling with infantile anguishes & anxieties."

Five years later, when Elizabeth came to live in Toronto for a year, we met up again, and we became close friends. It occurs to me now that in one afternoon she told me all I needed to know about obsessive passion, but of course I hadn't been able to hear her. It was only by following the strands of her life that I came to understand what she meant.

Elizabeth was born in 1913 into a wealthy Ottawa family. The money was mostly spent keeping up appearances: the elegant homes were rented. Mrs. Smart ran a formal household. There were so many rules about politeness and decorum that Elizabeth and her two sisters always claimed they were confused about how to behave at all. Mrs. Smart's fantasy was that her daughters would grow up to be the wives of diplomats. In this, they all disappointed her.

Elizabeth wanted to be a writer. She published her first poem at age ten in *Junior Home*, an American magazine, and was paid a dollar for it. By the time she was sixteen, she had printed and bound by hand *The Complete Works of Betty Smart*. In the bath, she would memorize the *Oxford Book of Modern Verse*.

But if she was to be a real writer, how was she to get started? She wrote in her diary: "Oh, for time to breathe, to live, to enjoy, to revolt, to be vulgar, to philosophize, to digest, to be flippant, to be irreverent, to feel, to know, to understand." What she needed was a great emotional experience. She decided she must fall in love.

From her late teens, Elizabeth began scouring Canada and England for what she called "the he." At twenty-three, she walked into a London bookstore and picked up a book of poetry by a young bohemian called George Barker. She was entranced. She checked the biographical blurb and found he was her age. She said to herself, "That's the one," and, without even having seen a photograph of him, she told her friends she was going to marry him and have his babies. The lover would be her life solution.

When she finally contacted Barker to buy his manuscripts, she was living at a remote writers' colony in Big Sur, California. It was 1940. He had taken a temporary teaching job in Japan, but the Japanese had begun bombing China and he needed to get out. He wrote to Elizabeth begging her to send money for two steamship tickets. It was the first hint she had that he was married.

The United States had not yet entered the Second World War, but foreigners were under suspicion, especially Brits of draft age who should have been fighting. Still, Elizabeth managed to get Barker a quota number and, with the help of fellow writers, to raise money for the tickets. In due course, he arrived with his wife, and he and Elizabeth met on July 19, 1940; both were twenty-seven. "I am standing on a corner in Monterey, waiting for the bus to come in, and all the muscles of my will are holding my terror to face the moment I most desire." So begins *Grand Central*, the distilled record of the first stages of their love affair.

The real impediment to their relationship, it turned out, was not that Barker was married—he would eventually have five "wives." Rather, he had adopted the persona of the hard-drinking, womanizing poet and was what might be described as congenitally incapable of fidelity. Barker found Elizabeth beautiful, yet he was not interested in being on the receiving end of her romantic obsession.

But she was working on an entirely different agenda. She saw love as a heroic myth—she and George were destined for each other. She believed in an exotic vision of what total love might be and that George Barker would come to see this too. How stubbornly she clung to her version through Barker's infidelities, his cruelties, his desertions. What was Elizabeth up to? How did she get so stuck?

It's too simple to see Elizabeth as a victim. In her own mind she was heroic, but to understand this requires an act of historical imagination. Elizabeth thought she was sabotaging the history of female passivity. Intoxicated by a vision of her own erotic power, she was taking the initiative. In her novel, the heroine is "virile as a cobra." "Eons have been evolving and planets disintegrating and forming to compel these two together," she writes. "I was born for this." She can no more resist her grand passion than "the earth can refuse the rain." The tone of the book is imperial, imperative, you might even say intolerant. "He is the one I picked out from the world ... in cold deliberation."

And the point is rebellion: "Love offends with its nudity." The word is to be posed against all those other words—*war, power, prudence, comfort*—thrust forward by the parade of taunting unbelievers. Love is sufficient to make the world anew. As readers, we are struck, even seduced, by the purity of her extremism.

The cultural norm of female passivity may seem a mere memory from a distant past, but it was the law in Elizabeth's world. How deeply engrained it was came to me only recently as I watched *Un homme et une femme*. I was shocked. I'd seen the film when I was in university in the late sixties. Then it had seemed so romantic.

The film has virtually no plot. A man and a woman meet. Anne works in films. Her husband, a stuntman, has recently died in an explosion during one of his stunts. Jean-Louis is a stock car racer. His wife committed suicide when she believed he had been killed in a crash.

The two pick up their respective children at boarding school. Nothing much happens. They spend a day together walking on the beach with their kids; they have dinner and drive to and from the rural boarding school. He disappears to race his car in the Monte Carlo rally. She works on a film. And then, when she sees him on television after the race, she sends a telegram that says: "Bravo! I love you. Anne."

When he reads the telegram, he gets up from his black-tie celebration dinner, jumps into his muddied stock car, and heads back to Paris. As he drives in the dark, we hear his thoughts (which I must admit sound a little more compelling in the original French): "To send a telegram like that. It's really something. You have to have guts to do that. Imagine. A beautiful woman sends a man a telegram like that. I'm not sure I'd have the guts to do it. It's extraordinary coming from a woman. Marvelous." He mulls over how to play this out. "When a woman sends you a telegram 'I love you,' you don't have to call first," he reassures himself. He imagines his arrival. "She'll be a little embarrassed, of course. After all, she just sent me a telegram saying: 'I love you.'"

It's hard to credit, such a fuss over a telegram. But a woman was never supposed to take the initiative. How could you trust her if she did?

Elizabeth believed she was heroic, picking the man she wanted with such delightful presumption. But George Barker, as one of her old friends put it, was a cad. Pregnant in 1941, Elizabeth fled to the West Coast of Canada to hide her disgrace. Meanwhile, her parents used their influence to have her lover barred from Canada on the grounds of "moral turpitude." After having her baby and writing her book, Elizabeth found work as a file clerk in the British army office in Washington. Barker was then in New York. There were "red nights under Brooklyn Bridge," but he was still living with his wife. At a time when civilian travel was severely restricted, Elizabeth managed to book passage to England. She was fleeing Barker and family. But he soon followed.

Three more children arrived in between his irregular visits. Elizabeth always said: "When George presented himself at the door, I'd try to kick him out, but then, he had such a good sense of humor." With amazing stamina, she brought up her children alone. It was not quite what she'd expected.

For the next fifteen years, Elizabeth worked in advertising and eventually became one of the best-paid copy writers in London. In the early 1960s she was literary editor at *Queen* magazine. The novelist Fay Weldon insisted Elizabeth changed the scene for women writers, giving them a leg up in a man's world.

But the price was her own writing. In the days when Elizabeth and I used to meet regularly at Dooney's Café on Bloor Street in Toronto, we talked about why. It wasn't only that it was hard to write and support her children at the same time, though this was certainly part of it. The most serious problem was that she had lost her nerve as a writer. She, who had dedicated her youth to obsessive love, confessed that she always felt a shadow was sitting on her shoulder. She called it the Maestro of the Masculine. It told her that she could never be good enough.

Elizabeth had a pretty good idea what had gone wrong. She had written her novel out of a wisdom she didn't know she possessed. Only years later did she realize that the man in her book was a true *love object*, a phantom she hardly knew. She fell in love not with the man but with the passion itself. He served as the training ground on which to crack open the defended self. Under the catalytic pressure of frustrated love, she discovered her own creative energies and wrote her book.

George Barker may have been the man Elizabeth loved most, but there were other lovers after him. As the father of her children he remained in her life, but eventually she could take him only in small doses. *He* hadn't destroyed her. It was the family drama she carried within that sabotaged her sense of self and made her blind to George's manipulations. Barker's last wife, who became a supportive friend, would say of Elizabeth after her death: "The spectre of your mother is always standing in your head one way or another. Elizabeth was always trying to prove to her mother that she could be loved."

The Tantalus love her mother offered, on her own terms, when her child behaved left Elizabeth with what she called that "whory" female need to please. So extreme was her mother's need for control that when her daughter's novel made it to Canada after the war, she bought up all the copies and burned them, and then tried to use her influence to get the prime minister to ban the book. Her daughter was sullying the family name, scandalously flaunting her adulterous love affair, and she didn't like the portrait of the mother in the book either.

Elizabeth was always trying to prove she was worthy of

someone's unconditional love. That's why she could demand so little, could settle for so little, and still call it love. She once said that what she most envied in George was his "roar of authority." He believed so totally in himself that he could sacrifice everything, including family and his own security, to his genius. She had never been able to put her own needs ahead of anyone's claims on her. This might have made her the better human being, but the cost was high. She described herself as having spent decades "lying low, earthquaked, deep frozen, mind askew." She called her only novella *Dig a Grave and Let Us Bury Our Mother*. She wanted different models, a wider range of possibilities for women to follow than the single template of the love story. In the end, she discovered that the one you mustn't betray is yourself.

17

Pleasurable Cruelty

She was almost disconcerted to discover he had a life.
He was very charismatic. She read the room. The way
certain women watched him, she could begin to imagine his
history, drawing lines between him and the women who
circled. He soon seemed to her like Gulliver tacked down by
endless strings.

When obsessive love takes over, we want the loved one
exclusively for ourselves for at least a year or twenty
years, alone in a room, a universe. Other people are
suddenly risky. Thoughts of our lover burst into everything. He becomes our world.

I recall a friend saying that unless there is jealousy, it
can't be love. Another possibility is that jealousy is particularly exaggerated when a relationship is imbalanced, and
the assurance of love one needs and has a right to expect
from the lover isn't forthcoming.

A young woman described to me her relationship with her lover. They had been together about a year and the tension was high. He was restless. They had reached an accommodation: they were lovers, they were friends; both were free to be with other people. At a party, they always acted as if they weren't together. One evening, she found herself being pursued by a pestering man and so sat down next to her lover at the table. He was annoyed, agitated. She got up and left the party. When she saw him next, she asked him if he had been jealous of the other man. He replied: "Actually, I was annoyed at you. I was just getting somewhere with that blonde across the table."

What is disturbing is that she accepted this deliberate cruelty. It didn't compromise her attachment to him. She still believed she loved him and that he loved her. He had always told her that he seduced unattractive women because they were no challenge. It was beautiful women like her who frightened him and made him feel insecure.

And so she attributed his behavior the power games that are inevitable in relationships. Yet she wouldn't have mistreated him this same way. What made it possible for him to feel good about himself, humiliating her like this? What made it possible for her to allow herself to be so treated?

I wonder whether we sometimes take an unexpected pleasure in being cruel. I was talking about this with an old friend and she recalled how she had once met a young man at her gym. She realized almost immediately that he was completely smitten with her; she could see the hunger in his eyes. Though she was flattered, for her the chemistry wasn't there. She went out with him a few times, but when he asked her to meet him at a bar one night and something else came up, she felt no compunction at the idea of standing him up. She realized she even felt contempt for his hang-dog love because she was sure nothing she could do would change his obsessing over her. When she examined this pleasurable cruelty, she thought, with alarm, that she was behaving like those men who are cruel to the women who love them and who will do just enough to keep them hanging around. It's more than the flattery they like. It's the power.

My friend discovered that we can feel contempt for those who give us power over them by loving us too much. She kept her appointment with the young man. And it turned out she was wrong. She told me there *was* something she could do to change his obsessing over her. She stopped playing with his feelings.

18

Don Juan / Doña Juana

*One woman in particular unnerved her, greeting Varian as
though publicly staking a claim.*

In the age-old cliché, a man will fight over a woman as if
she were the prize trophy. But a woman will compete
against another woman for the prize in a ruthless, predatory way.

Anyone who has been involved in a triangular affair
knows how this works. Neither our own motives nor our
man's are examined. The other woman is the enemy. She
must be defeated.

What kind of man precipitates such acrimony? Tradi-
tionally, the man who indulges in multiple lovers is a Don
Juan archetype, a narcissist. And what characterizes a
narcissist is that the only real relationship he is capable of
is one with himself.

The novelist Leon Whiteson once remarked that most

men who play this role do so to cover their fear of intimacy. "SIN for men," he explained, "is Safety In Numbers." Having many women is a guarantee against having to deal intimately with one individual woman. It's a perfect device for protecting the bottom line: *I need no one.* As soon as such a man allows himself to acknowledge need, he opens himself to betrayal. How can he trust that he will not be abandoned?

The bad luck for women is that we often find men who fit the Don Juan archetype to be so attractive. They fall impulsively into erotic relationships, and we women immediately get ourselves busy searching out the heart within these transparently sensitive men. We do not recognize that their whole strategy is to keep us unsettled: now you know him, now you don't. This kind of man can't deal with women candidly because to do so would compromise his power. And for us, the not-knowing, the continual shift in his affections, leaves us in a state of constant anxiety and self-doubt.

These affairs can only degenerate into very unpleasant Tantalus games. The dynamic is thoroughly destructive, a push/pull dance of misinterpretation. Nights of hysteria without sleep. Days plotting what to say. Then the accusatory barbs. A woman will find herself trivialized, undermined. She turns into the very thing she hates most: the supplicating female.

So much of obsessive love takes place in the head. We spend our time desperately trying to understand the other's perspective. It's as if we have failed a test we had no idea we were taking. We want to justify ourselves, to have our interpretation heard. We are left with lingering feelings of failure and guilt. We haven't the least clue what's going on.

I have been speaking as if there were no female equivalent to Don Juan, but of course there is a Doña Juana, though she hasn't been so named. She is variously called the *femme fatale*, the seductress, the siren, the vamp, *la Belle Dame Sans Merci*.

One of her most fascinating incarnations is as Scarlett O'Hara in the 1939 film *Gone With the Wind*. Scarlett is petulant, childish, totally limited in her feelings, and seemingly irresistible to men. She collects men as trophies for her beauty, using them for her own ends. She admits to having no real feeling for them and complains about the need to pretend she does. As a type, her power is incomprehensible to women. She is so transparent; can't men see through her?

But the quality of the seductress that is irresistible to men is her combination of vulnerability and willfulness. She has a passionate energy, an infectious appetite for life (Scarlett's favorite expletive is "great balls of fire"), but she trades on her helplessness. Probably men are flattered, but not fooled. They secretly admire her strength, which is, paradoxically, so unfeminine. One lover complains, with relish, that she cut her teeth on his heart.

Scarlett is ruthless, self-absorbed and manipulative. As

the film makes clear, war brings out the best in her—her indomitable will to survive. She lies, cheats, and even steals her sister's fiancé to keep the family estate intact. At war's end, knowing there will be a building boom, she sets up her own lumber business and is as brutal as any man, replacing slave labor with that of convicts on starvation rations.

But while the Don Juan is often admired by other men for his swordsmanship (that old metaphor for sexual conquest), the vamp is vilified by other women for throwing herself after men, for making a spectacle of herself, and so forth. She becomes an outsider, and the only one to whom she might be vulnerable is an outsider like herself.

In *Gone With the Wind*, Rhett Butler is the outsider, and Scarlett's twin. He says they're made for each other—they're both selfish and ruthless, but, as he once remarks, at least they have the guts to look life in the face.

The vamp, like the Don Juan, is always the basis for a cautionary tale and both must get their comeuppance. By the end of the film, Scarlett discovers she really loves Rhett Butler, but it's too late. His cavalier dismissal of her final plea to stay is the stuff of legend. And he's a smart man not to give in. To do so would be foolish. He knows Scarlett's misfortune is to love only the one who resists her. After all, he's a Don Juan himself.

These days we are less prescriptive in our notions of sexual propriety, and so the seducers and seductresses are not nearly so coy in their behavior. And anyway, at some point most of us play at erotic games of seduction and many of us are even promiscuous. But the game of sexual conquest can still involve a cautionary tale.

To play at sex hardens the heart. *Why can't I meet anyone who feels anything?* we say. *Why can't I meet anyone who responds?* Yet sometimes what we are meaning is the exact opposite: *Why can't I let myself go, and love?*

19

Erotic Diabolism

The woman who'd so obviously claimed him at the party
entered carrying two oranges. When she saw the two of them,
she set down the oranges carefully: "I should have known I
would need to bring three," she said. "Let me see her." Exas-
perated, Varian threw back the covers, exposing their
naked bodies. ...

She was surprised that, instead of being angry, she was
aroused. She felt as though she'd woken up in a French film.

A friend of mine, Marlene Goldman, coined a phrase I
like: erotic diabolism. She means to convey that we play
at the dangerous, the diabolical in erotic games. The
example in my story is a mild one: a young woman is
getting off on the brief thrill of exhibitionism.

But what underlies it? Two women are fighting over a
man. They are competitors for the prize. The winner

enjoys her rival's defeat and humiliation. If either stopped for a second and extricated herself from the scene, she would see the cruelty they've been drawn into. But each is obsessed. Each is enclosed in her own solipsistic bubble.

In my story, I wanted to replicate one of those moments when we get things exactly wrong. I was imagining my character in bed with her lover when she hears the key turn in the door and the woman she recognizes from the party arrives with a gift. It had to be something the woman brought for herself and the man: two oranges. When the woman sees the man in bed with another, instead of being shocked she says wearily, "I should have brought three."

What my character cannot hear is the tone of voice of the other woman. Had she been really listening, she would have recognized that this is a familiar moment. It is not the first time the woman has found this man in bed with someone else. But my character is too blinded by her obsession to realize that this particular man is used to being in the middle of such sexual tugs-of-war. Though he accepts no responsibility for precipitating this scene, he has actually set it up by giving his apartment key to the woman. It is not the gesture of intimacy it should be. It does not guarantee that she will find his bed empty. But his cruelty is casual. He does this because he can get away with it, since no one calls him on it.

And my character feels a sense of victory, since the lover returns to her bed. She does not see that she is being used against another woman, nor how the other woman is humiliated. But then, she is needy, and ruthless in her own way.

My friend Laurie Maher tells me that sometimes she feels we are beings that morph, like balls of mercury or like amoebas. We float around until we find something to attach ourselves to. Once we attach and absorb, it's almost like we've been chemically altered. Then the intensity lessens, as though the thing we needed is chemical. "What's the chemical for confidence?" she asks me. By attaching herself obsessively to somebody else, she gets a sense of finally being competent in the world. "I'm jealous of people who have a good relationship with themselves," she says. She tells me about a children's fantasy film, *The Dark Crystal*, about beings that are drained of their essence by another entity. Whenever they try to detach themselves, that being reasserts its power. "When you're obsessed with someone and you try to leave," she explains, "you always get pulled back in."

Why do we sanitize erotic passion with sentimental images of hearts and flowers when it flips so easily into its dark side? The line between what I have been calling erotic diabolism and something more sinister is thin—the one can slip into the other without our noticing.

One thing is certain. When overwhelmed by obsessive love, we are hooked on the drama of intensity. Later, though, as boredom and familiarity grow, the word *passion* too often reverts to its root meaning, suffering.

20

Two Solitudes Meet

And then, with no further reference to what had occurred, he told her of the dream he'd had earlier, before the woman intruded. He was standing outside an apartment house in an abandoned city. A man invited him inside. As he wandered from room to room, a strange carnival was under way. He was led to a woman sitting serenely like a Buddha, but when the woman's cloak fell away, she had two rows of little breasts that ended not in nipples but in bird beaks.

I'm talking about that heady stage in a love affair that feels like mutuality but is, in fact, two solitudes meeting. Each person thinks they know what the other is thinking, but they are mistaken. The truth is, at this moment each is caught up in his or her own needs.

As he proceeds to recount his dream, the man in my story is absorbed only in his own drama. The woman doesn't even notice this. In fact, she never really hears him since she is listening only for clues to his feelings about her.

Dreams rip away any pretense of civility. I want this moment to reveal how afraid my male character is of relationships. In his dream, the nurturing breast turns into bird beaks. He knows that, even though they pretend to feed and to soothe, women are really predators. They feed off you. He is afraid that he will be consumed. And in a way, he's right. He is not a *person* for this woman but a fantasy she needs to complete something in herself.

I am sitting in a lovely Italian restaurant on Yonge Street with two friends, Joan Peterson and Arlene Lampert. The sun is bearing down on the patio but we don't notice because we are absorbed in a puzzle: do men and women love differently? We reach the conclusion that men get their power from possessing and women from being possessed. Arlene says, "That's why when it breaks up, *he* says: 'How dare you leave me,' while *she* thinks, 'What did I do wrong?'" And then we laugh. We are so quick to reach for generalizations.

Why? I suppose this comes not just from personal experience but also from inherited wounds between the sexes that have yet to heal. I was intrigued by an essay by the poet Anne Carson called "Dirt and Desire." She writes about the way women were viewed as polluters in ancient Greece. The Greeks believed that civilization depended on boundaries, which guaranteed order. Because they were potential violators of male boundaries, women were regarded as dangerous and in need of control.

The Greeks viewed woman as a "mobile unit." She was moved from her father's house to her husband's house. Regrettably, however, she was also capable of self-propulsion, of illicit (i.e., adulterous) movement. In order to control women, to isolate and insulate them, the Greeks developed a theory of the polluting effects of women and a code of conduct for pollution control. In his book *Works and Days*, the Greek poet Hesiod advised, "Let a man not clean his skin in water that a woman has washed in. For a hard penalty follows on that for a long time." (It was not only the Greeks who had such proscriptions; many of the same fetishes about female uncleanliness can be found in Christian, Jewish, and Muslim traditions.)

Women were perceived as polluters because, as Carson discovered, "physiologically and psychologically women are wet," whereas men are dry. Aristotle explained this difference anatomically: the male fetus leans to the right, whereas the female fetus leans to the left, and the "right side of the body is hotter than the left." That which is wet has no boundaries and can readily violate other boundaries. That which is dry is already bounded by itself. The problem with women is that they swell and shrink. They leak. They can't or won't stay within their own boundaries; they keep flowing into men. Men, on the other hand, are bounded and rational and they are capable of self-control.

As Carson warns us, it pays to remember that in Greek mythology the goddess of love, Aphrodite, was born from the castration of the god Uranus when the blood of his severed penis fertilized the sea. Women's eroticism was believed to be fearsome, rapacious. Of all the emotions, by far the most dangerous for a man was erotic desire, for it drowned the mind. A man could become delusional when trapped in a woman's body and lose himself. Greek civilization depended on men being capable of resisting female assaults on their psychological boundaries.

I like Carson's essay because it goes beyond the usual explanation of patriarchy's need to control women: namely, that this need is based solely on systems of property; that because men must be assured the legitimacy of their progeny, women must be owned.

But added to this is fear. To desire another makes one vulnerable and involves great risk. One can lose one's bearings. Better to keep woman at a distance or under lock and key. The problem is that men keep falling in love with women and losing their safe boundaries.

21

Self-Portrait with Mirrors

His dream reeled her in tighter. What had it to do with her?
Did he see her as the dream catcher who could help him to
change? Was this some kind of appeal? Clearly he felt
compelled by her if he could offer her these broken shards of his
life.

I ask myself what enables a woman to take a rejection and
turn it into an appeal.

Her lover's look of contempt had effaced this woman,
undermined her sense of herself. While he got angry, she
was thinking, "What happened? What have I done
wrong?" But when he relates his dream, she gets a chance
to recover. She assumes that he is telling it to her because
it has something to do with her; he must be asking her for
something. What must she do to keep this man?

The inner dialogue never ceases. She thinks it's her

responsibility to be perfect. This is a perverse form of narcissism, this continuous picking over of one's own plumage. She does not yet know that real love does not demand perfection. To prove she is worthy, he becomes her project. She will assume responsibility for his happiness, whether he wants it or not.

I am fascinated with female narcissism. We think of narcissism as self-love, but it is actually self-obsession. At its most extreme, it means being so trapped in a battle between self-hatred and self-love that the outside world ceases to exist except with reference to oneself. Every woman knows this battle, if only in a minor way. We are encouraged to fall in love with our own image, but then we can never be beautiful enough. Endlessly self-conscious, we assume the world is always watching and judging when, in fact, the world is indifferent to our small fates.

A perfect example of the conundrum of female narcissism is the Mexican painter Frida Kahlo. Kahlo became an icon in the 1980s, almost thirty years after her death. Her face graced posters and calendars, and everywhere there were exhibitions of her work. Like pilgrims, groupies flocked to her house in San Angel, Mexico City, which was crammed full of memorabilia. It was reported that Madonna was spending millions to buy her paintings.

Frida Kahlo was born in 1907 (though she always put 1910 on her passport). Her father, Guillermo, was a successful photographer hired by the dictator Porfirio

Díaz to travel throughout Mexico, recording its architectural heritage. Her mother, Matilde Calderón, was a devout Catholic.

From childhood, Frida was betrayed by her body. Bedridden for nine months with polio at the age of six, she hated the withered leg that resulted from the illness. Aggressively, she turned looking different into a virtue. At fourteen, she cut her hair short—to offend the bourgeois mothers of her classmates. Loving male camouflage, she took to wearing a man's suit and tie and roamed the streets of her native Coyoacán (a suburb of Mexico City) imitating the language of bootblacks and street vendors. She was her father's favorite and followed him about as he photographed the city's churches and monuments. He too was wounded. He suffered from epileptic fits, and on their excursions, she always carried a bottle of ether to be used if he had an attack.

When Frida was fourteen, the great Mexican painter Diego Rivera was hired to paint murals at her school, and as she watched him on the high scaffold, she assured her school chums she would be his lover: "My ambition is to have a child by Diego Rivera. And I'm going to tell him so someday."

In 1925 Frida's life changed forever when a bus on which she was traveling was hit by a trolley car. The handrail above her head broke loose and pierced her body, fracturing her pelvis and several vertebrae and irreparably damaging her foot. For the first month after the accident, her doctors were not certain she would live. Miraculously, she was walking again within three months, but she continued to suffer relapses. It was during one of her long confinements to bed that she began to paint. As her biographer Hayden Herrera explained, from the time of her accident Frida's life became "a grueling battle against slow decay." She had at least thirty-two operations before she died at the age of forty-seven.

In 1928, Frida finally met Rivera at a party at the home of the bohemian photographer Tina Modotti. But the "official" version she recorded was that they met when she called him down from his scaffold at the Ministry of Education where he was painting frescoes and demanded that he assess her artistic talent. "Diego, come down!" she shouted up, and he descended the ladder. "Look," she claims to have said, "I have not come to flirt or anything even if you are a woman-chaser. I have come to show you my painting. If you are interested in it, tell me so, if not, likewise, so that I will go to work at something else to help my parents." She had enormous pride and erotic confidence. This was a performance. Willful and acquisitive, if naive, she was certain she could win him. And she did.

Already separated from his first wife, Rivera married Frida in 1929. He was forty-three; she was twenty years younger. He was notoriously ugly. Frida's family remarked: "It was like an elephant marrying a dove."

At the wedding, his ex-wife, Lupe Marín Rivera,

reportedly strode up to Frida, lifted high the bride's skirt, and shouted to the assembled guests: "You see these two sticks? These are the legs Diego has now instead of mine!" Frida described the post-wedding party. "Diego went on such a terrifying drunken binge with tequila that he took out his pistol, he broke a man's little finger, and broke other things. Then we had a fight, and I left crying and went home."

Rivera was already Mexico's most famous—and infamous—artist. There were legends of him laboring for days on his scaffold, regaling onlookers and friends with fictitious tales of his fighting in the Russian Revolution. Frida, dressed in Tehuantepec costume like an archetype from a Rivera painting, would arrive carrying lavish picnic lunches in baskets covered with flowers. Being married to him was a full-time job. He was one of those epic artists who boasted of their artistic harems, and soon Frida was keeping a file of letters labeled "From Diego's Women." She adored him even when she hated him.

Frida once said to a friend, "I have suffered two serious accidents in my life, one in which a streetcar ran over me. ... The other accident is Diego." Her self-portraits are full of blood that seeps even onto the frames of the paintings. And canvas after canvas is a self-portrait. When asked why she painted herself so often, she replied: "Because I am alone."

A painter I know, Rae Johnson, has painted the same pond outside her window innumerable times. She has painted it in all seasons, all lights, all hours of the day. She loves the idea of the minuscule change that alters everything: the butterfly's fluttering wing on the other side of the world that starts a tidal wave. It's obsessive, claustrophobic, and profound.

What was Frida doing painting her own face with the same obsessive intensity? Her costumes change, but the face rarely does. She doesn't age; she looks with the same passivity at the viewer, over and over. Sometimes a miniature portrait of Rivera, like a cameo, appears as a third eye in the middle of her forehead. She is like an icon on canvas.

What is she saying? That the female self is a performance? That she exists only in the reflected look of others? Or was she, always so close to pain and death, simply holding on to herself? It's impossible to know, of course. But to me it is as if she is caught in the female self: her beauty is a gift; it is also a snare, a trap.

In the world of animals it is usually the males that are beautiful. In the aviary of a botanical garden in Dijon, I came across a large cage in which an exquisite tropical bird (there was no indication of its name or breed) strutted back and forth, stopping occasionally to preen its peacock-like tail. It suddenly occurred to me that in nature, beauty is a liability. It takes courage to be beautiful, to turn oneself into a target. While the female bird rested tranquilly in the sun grooming inconspicuously, he strutted exposed, demanding attention. What could possibly have been more beautiful than this bird with its sun yellow crest, its cerulean breast and teal beak? But beauty was beside the point. He was drawing the fire: Look here, not there. Poor bird, he was kept unnamed in a cage because he was too beautiful.

For humans, beauty can also be a constraint. Frida believed her beauty kept Rivera; her native dress was a performance initially donned for him. But when she found out he had seduced her sister, the world fell apart. She expressed her despair by symbolically destroying her female beauty: she cut her hair off. She did this again in 1940, after another of Rivera's erotic liaisons, and painted *Self-Portrait with Cropped Hair*. In the painting, she sits in a bright yellow chair wearing one of Rivera's oversized suits, her legs spread apart like a man's. Above her head is the caption: "Look if I loved you it was for your hair. Now that you have cut it, I don't love you any more."

Frida's life with Rivera was extreme, but it was this very extremism that was the addiction. She celebrated romantic obsession. Idolatry; I adore him. Frida said, "I love Diego more than my own skin." When he abandoned her, she felt completely effaced.

In 1939, Frida and Diego divorced, but a year later they remarried and moved back to Coyoacán. Rivera still kept a bedroom for himself in another suburb, but Frida was training herself to take his erotic love interests less seriously. She too had her own lovers, male and female, but more important, she painted her despair, and now painting was her life.

She freed herself, more or less, from her dependency on Diego, from her need to have him invent her with his praise. And she had also freed him: "Why do I call him my Diego?" she wrote. "He belongs to himself."

It took everything she had in her to survive Diego Rivera—not the man but the idol she had made him into. At her last exhibition, to which she was taken on a stretcher by ambulance with a motorcycle escort, she said, "I am not sick. I am broken. But I am happy to be alive as long as I can paint."

It's not surprising that the pop diva Madonna would fall in love with Frida Kahlo's paintings. If she had been a painter, she, too, would probably have painted only self-portraits. Her concerts have always been theatrical, with herself as the subject—as an Amazon with steel tits jutting from her armored breastplate or a madonna who seduces the man on the cross. It was parody, of course, but clever and gutsy.

The critic Camille Paglia has talked about Madonna's brilliant "fabrications of femininity," her multiple sexual personae, from the cross-dressing dominatrix to the slave of male desire. She claims that Madonna recovered the power of the virgin harlot, the pagan whore who ruled over man.

A clearer analysis, it seems to me, is offered by Madonna's own 1992 autobiographical film, *Truth or Dare*. What I find most disturbing about that film is Madonna's solipsism. She appears to believe everyone is out to use her, to leech her power. She allows no one to approach her except subordinates. Two men stand on the periphery: her lover at the time, Warren Beatty, appalled by her narcissism, and the father whom she treats with incestuous contempt.

Madonna turned herself into one of the most powerful and profitable business tycoons in Hollywood. But the archetype she presented to young women, while it may have worked on celluloid, is not helpful in the real world. Without Madonna's millions, the virgin/whore is as powerless in the face of male exploitation as she has always been.

Perhaps what *is* helpful is Madonna's absolute refusal of female guilt, of the sense of being constrained by what others think. For her, femaleness is a performance: you can rearrange yourself, you can change your presentation with costumes and disguises. It's *your* terms for *your* life.

Madonna's insistence on controlling her sexuality may also be a very important lesson. The thing to be learned is that if you are playing these games, you must refuse to be objectified, to be limited to being a sex object. Few women really believe the degree to which some men objectify them; most are certainly incapable of returning the favor.

I was reading an article in a woman's magazine by a

female reporter whose assignment was to find and date a male escort, all expenses paid. She eventually discovered twenty-seven-year-old Craig on the Internet. Craig explained that he didn't like having sex on the first date. "If someone wanted me just for sex," he said, "they would have to pay a lot more than $100 an hour." Women hired him for companionship, for someone to talk to or to go to the theater with. Sometimes they wanted to use him to make an old boyfriend jealous or take revenge on a cheating husband. Of the two hundred or three hundred women he had dated, he said he went the "horizontal distance" with about thirty.

But it was really the woman reporter who fascinated me. She concluded her article with the complaint that ordering sex was too cold-blooded. The problem was a male escort's flattering comments wouldn't be sincere. "Women have their female antennae so well tuned to male insincerity ... how could I know whether he finds me attractive? Asking straight out wouldn't help—I would never believe him if he said yes."

When a man hires a female escort, he calls the shots, at least within limits. And when he's the one hired, that doesn't seem to jeopardize his sense of power. He's still in control. At least in this case, the female reporter is still preoccupied with her attractiveness. Hunting for validation and approval, she gives over to the man the power to reject her. She has no idea how silly she appears, submitting her sense of self-esteem to a cocky callboy.

22

The Silver Screen

At times she found herself walking aimlessly through the streets of Mexico. It was the most exciting city in the world, and yet for her it now had the indecipherable vagueness of a dream. At moments, the whole affair seemed ridiculous—dead men in cafés, women with oranges. She felt as though she were participating in some kind of dress rehearsal. There was something she was trying to get right. But what?

Nothing is more claustrophobic than a love affair. Our whole energy is focused on our obsession and we cease to function in the world. The obsession brings an astounding intensity, but nothing else is left of life. It is so overwhelming because suddenly we are plunged into the full range of human passion, from agony to ecstasy and back again. We yearn to stand up against all that stops us from reaching the full stretch of ourselves and our desires.

But we confuse this yearning with the qualities of the

lover. So absorbed are we in our own drama, so inflated with a sense of love's colossal power, that we can't imagine he is not caught up in this too. If not, he must be willfully blind. We must make him see. Doesn't he realize we have been willing to risk everything? At least everything but our own version of how things are?

But then, where does that version come from? What is the script for obsessive love, and who writes it?

In 1939, on the eve of the Second World War, a film called *Love Affair*, directed by Leo McCarey and starring Charles Boyer and Irene Dunne, became an instant classic. I doubt that any other film has been remade as often. In 1957, McCarey redid his own film as *An Affair to Remember*, starring Cary Grant and Deborah Kerr. In 1994, reverting to the old title *Love Affair*, Warren Beatty produced an updated version starring himself and Annette Bening. And in 1993, Nora Ephron wrote and directed *Sleepless in Seattle*, which centers on characters who watch and in part relive *An Affair to Remember*. What's so intriguing about this love plot that it should keep coming back?

In *Sleepless in Seattle*, Ephron identifies the hook: if two people are made for each other, they will find each other despite distance, time, and common sense. The film opens with Ephron's character Annie trying on her wedding dress as her mother looks on. Her mother claims to believe in destiny; Annie is cynical. Then destiny intervenes and changes the course of her life. By chance, hearing a guy speak of his love for his dead wife on a radio talk show, Annie drops her dullard of a boyfriend and heads to Seattle to hunt him down. The film suggests that the fantasy that events are meaningful signs and not just coincidences is indestructible.

There's a comic scene when the characters sit at a kitchen table and discuss *An Affair to Remember*. The guys insist that it's a chick flick, and they make fun of the female character by retelling the plot of *The Dirty Dozen* while bawling their eyes out. And it's true, every female in the film, from Annie to a ten-year-old girl, watches *An Affair to Remember* and bawls her eyes out. Are we just sentimentalists, or is something else going on?

I think the answer lies in the original film and its 1957 remake. It's not a chick flick at all. It's a male fantasy.

The scripts of the original *Love Affair* and its first remake are largely the same, except for a few minor details. For instance, the Frenchman, Michel, becomes the Italian-American, Nicky, probably to accommodate the metamorphosis of the lead from the seductive Boyer to the fast-talking Grant. The soundtracks, however, differ completely. In the original, the theme song is the exquisite "Plaisir d'Amour"; in the remake, it is the sentimental "An Affair to Remember," sung by Vic Damone. Which version you prefer probably depends on whether you find the sultry Boyer or the ironic and ebullient Grant more seductive.

The plot is simple. A couple meet on an ocean liner. He,

a notorious and extravagant playboy, is going to meet his wealthy fiancée, an American millionairess. She, a former nightclub singer, is also returning to her fiancé, who keeps her in a penthouse on Park Avenue in a style to which she has become accustomed. Meeting by chance, they are seduced by each other's witty repartee. When he invites her into his stateroom, she demurs with the wonderful line, "It's not that I'm prudish, but my mother told me never to enter a man's room in months ending in 'r.'" And then she invites him into *her* stateroom. He tells her that she's the first beautiful woman he's seen on board, and she laughs at the transparency of his come-on, adding, "I do hope this [rejection] won't affect your ego." "Don't think anything of it. I'll just take my ego for a walk," he replies, "unless, of course, you'd care to ..." "Have dinner? I'd love to." She has already begun to finish his sentences.

The chemistry works, and suddenly they are heading into "a rough sea." Each knows that the other loves money. Will love be enough to give up comfort? He says: "I've never done a day's work in my whole life. Expensive furs, diamonds, pink champagne. That's the kind of life we've both been used to." "Do you like beer?" she asks skeptically, admitting this could be difficult. (It's fascinating how often we oppose love and money, as if we live in constant bad faith about the guilty pleasures of materialism. In the old myths, love always made the pauper into the prince.)

Finally, he takes the plunge: "If I worked hard enough and long enough, say six months, where would you be?"

She's puzzled: "What are you trying to say, Nicky?" His voice cracking, he replies, "I just want to be worthy of asking you to marry me." They decide to sleep on it, separately.

As they are about to disembark in New York the next morning, she gives him a note: "Darling, you have a date, my beloved, July first at five o'clock." He counters: "But you don't say where?" She responds: "Well, you name the place and I'll obey." He looks up: "Top of the Empire State Building." She adds impulsively, "The nearest thing to heaven we have in New York." It's a test. If one doesn't show, the other is not allowed to ask why.

As I said, this film is a male fantasy, and the real core of *Love Affair* occurs in the middle of the film when the ship docks for several hours and the man who is falling in love with the woman takes her to meet his grandmother. This is necessary to the plot for two reasons. We must have a model of "true" love. The grandmother, at eighty-two with a dog called Fidèle (in case we missed the point), remains faithful to the memory of her dead husband, praying every day in the private chapel where he lies buried. And she gets to tell the young woman what's wrong with her grandson: "There is nothing wrong with Nicolo that a good woman couldn't make right."

We discover Nicky is a failed artist. Grandma instinctively knows this girl has the right stuff. She tells her that she is worried about her grandson: "What the artist in him would create, the critic would destroy." He's now too busy living. Painting, piano playing, everything comes too easily. "He's always attracted by the art he isn't practicing, the place he hasn't been, the girl he hasn't met." And there we have it. It's the male fantasy: love is the route to living the life he hasn't had the courage to choose. And she's the muse whose love allows him to finally believe in himself.

And indeed that's what happens. During the six months before the appointed reunion, he turns himself into a successful painter. She leaves her boyfriend and goes back to singing in a nightclub, but not with a career in mind. She's waiting for him to get his act together. What follows is one of the most famous moments in cinema. On the day of their rendezvous, as she dashes from the taxi to get to the Empire State Building, the driver asks her what's the rush. She replies: "I'm going to be married." She disappears from the screen and then there's the horrific thud of metal hitting a body. In the next clip, she's delirious in hospital and he's atop the Empire State angrily pacing as thunder and lightning hammer the night sky.

Obviously Leo McCarey remade his film because he knew he had a good thing going. *Love Affair* had been so successful that, eighteen years later, it made commercial sense to update it starring Hollywood's new heartthrob, Cary Grant. But there is one change in the script that I find interesting, as if McCarey decided to be a little more precise on this go-round. It's an odd little scene that occurs months after the failed reunion. Cary Grant's art dealer and mentor, Corbet, visits his studio to look at his work. Examining each picture, Corbet says, "I can read your state of mind when you painted these. You were very sorry for yourself when you painted this one. You were angry here. You were getting over your broken heart. Here you became a painter."

Suffering makes the artist. For the man, the love story is a route to something else, in this case his own creativity and confidence. Falling in love, he finds his own emotional range. And meanwhile, what has become of the female lead? She's in an orphanage, teaching music from her wheelchair.

Then there's the famous last scene when he comes to visit her in her apartment. She lies demurely on the sofa. "There must be something between us," he says, "even if it's only an ocean." He's sailing that night for Europe. Like the mythic Flying Dutchman, he intends to keep sailing because he can't get over her betrayal. He has no idea that she's paralyzed, and, fearing his love will turn to pity, she says nothing. Suddenly he remembers that his dealer spoke of giving one of his paintings to a crippled girl, and there it is on the wall in an adjacent room. He asks, "Why didn't you tell me?"

"It was nobody's fault but my own," she replies. "I was looking up at the nearest thing to heaven, and you were there."

The last words of the film are extraordinary: "Don't

worry," she says. "If you can paint, I can walk." It's a fair exchange: he gets to do what he most deeply wants; she gets to walk.

Warren Beatty's remake of *Love Affair* was a failure, though it's amusing for anyone who knows the older versions. The lovers—he's an aging American playboy called Michael who was once a football star and she's her boss's mistress—meet on a plane from New York to Australia. When their plane is forced to make an emergency landing on an atoll, a Russian cruise ship saves them and the shipboard romance begins. The script isn't exactly scintillating. She remarks that she has a weakness for nice things. He replies that nice things are nice.

The plot is essentially the same, though the dialogue has been updated. Michael confesses he's never been faithful to any woman in his life, and he wonders how she will ever trust him. When he asks for time to get a job and put his life in order, she gives him three months. Who can wait six months these days?

But if the writing's flat, at least Beatty understands that what's at stake is passion, wanting something badly enough and having the courage to take it. Love is again the catalyst by which Michael finds the nerve to change his life. He's going to coach football and paint in his spare time. She still gets hit by a car.

The *Sleepless in Seattle* update involves a whole new component. Suddenly, it's a film written and directed by a woman. We might expect a simple inversion of the original plot, whereby the woman is the one redeemed by the man's love, but instead the film is caught hopelessly in a schizophrenic tug between cynicism and romantic longing. The characters watch Cary Grant and Deborah Kerr on video, while the film is threaded with such sentimental love songs as "Make Someone Happy," "As Time Goes By," "Stardust," "In the Wee Small Hours of the Morning," and "A Kiss to Build a Dream On." Ephron is clearly asking: How does popular culture shape our expectations? And are there still such things as destiny and magic?

Dr. Marcia Fieldstone hosts a radio talk show called *You and Your Emotions*, and the subject under discussion Christmas Eve is "Wishes and Dreams." A child, whose mother died eighteen months earlier, phones in and says his father is sad and he needs a wife. The father, Sam Baldwin, played by Tom Hanks, gets on the phone, and Dr. Fieldstone manipulates him into describing his love for the woman he's lost. Two thousand women call in asking for his phone number.

Annie, a Baltimore journalist played by Meg Ryan, has heard the program and tells her office colleagues. The males dismiss the callers as middle-aged women desperate for love. But romantic longing has caught Annie and she becomes obsessed.

This film starts as a send-up of *An Affair to Remember*. All the characters share a modern cynicism about fate and the perfect match. The perfect match is two neuroses meeting:

147

when the rocks in his head fit the holes in hers. For Sam, fate, where everything intersects, is the Bermuda Triangle.

But Ephron won't quite give up on destiny. She rewrites the script. This time the male lover isn't the one who sets up the rendezvous; instead, it's the eight-year-old boy. The radio show has been forwarding listener mail to him. Having received a letter from Annie, he knows she's the right one and arranges to meet her at the top of the Empire State Building. Alone, he flies across the country to meet destiny. When the taxi driver asks him why he's in such a rush, he replies that he's going to meet his new mother. Thank god *he* doesn't have to get hit by a truck.

Annie arrives at the Empire State Building late. To persuade the guard to let her up after the elevators have closed, she says that there's someone waiting for her and if she doesn't take a look she'll never know if she missed her fate. The guard says he's seen the film.

Sleepless in Seattle is a feel-good button-pusher. The destiny-lends-a-hand meeting is comic farce. Even if American kids are precocious little brats, what eight-year-old could make it to New York without walking into danger? It's charming, it's schmaltzy, and there are a number of good one-liners. As Sam and Annie, mesmerized by each other, get into the elevator with the child and the credits roll, we hear Celine Dion and Clive Griffin singing, "When I Fall in Love." We are invited to believe, if only for a moment, in the myth of *love ever after*, but then, look who's singing the song.

I remember Dion's horrific parody performance of *love ever after* in Las Vegas in 1999 when she publicly renewed her marriage vows with her husband, René Angélil, the man who has managed her career since she was twelve years old. As he sat in his sultan's costume, she was carried to him on a litter decked out like a Disneyland Cleopatra. The staged iconography of the erotic couple was grotesque.

Love is dangerous for women when it must be maintained as a performance. Ironically, it's the persistence of the fantasy of eternal love that undermines the improvisation needed to sustain a loving relationship. If Celine Dion is the model, it's time for us to rethink the female version of the love story.

23

Grief

Her pain filled all of Mexico City. She had been sliced open.
Alone in her hotel room, she found herself bellowing like an
animal. A piece of her was being ripped out. She let it happen.

Grief. Anguish. They are the definitive, the right words
for this. The pain is so extreme. It is a shattering experience, a terrifying longing that wrenches the gut. We can
find ourselves curled fetus-like, sobbing uncontrollably,
as if the world were ending. There is something
absolutely childlike about this sense of abandonment.

We have handed over our entire sense of ourselves to
someone else. We have let their belief in us or disap-
proval of us overwhelm our own feelings of worthiness.
Then love is brutally ripped away. No wonder we feel
lost. But there is something of great importance to be
learned. We are not destroyed.

What brings us to the point where we feel empty and

effaced? The panic, the hot congestion in the chest, the terror of an annihilating loss can happen only when we submerge ourselves in another.

I have gone back to read my old diaries—a quarter of a century back. I well remember that young girl who appears in those pages. I was trying so hard to get my life started. I wrote: "There are blind alleys that lead nowhere, something one finds out only after risking everything by traveling down them." I had fallen in love and it was going badly.

I had been married at twenty-one. Like Sylvia Plath's heroine, I lived under a bell jar, pretending to be in a perfect union. But peace is bought at a high price: anesthesia. If the feelings were too hard, I just didn't feel. I had allowed my emotional life to be taken over and structured by someone else. How was it possible to have my initiative taken away? How was it possible for me to give it up so easily?

This is one of my diary entries:

The definition of loneliness might be a couple at night, awake, turning incessantly in search of a solace that cannot be satisfied by any physical comfort, the exact position in the bed where anxiety might disappear. Both awake, knowing or intuiting the wakefulness of the other yet neither speaking. I reached to touch him with my hand and found my hand trapped by the blanket; the single bed I had forgotten I lay in embodied my separateness. My hand had moved of its own will like an animal, one of the blind and fearful small, groping in the darkness. The sadness I felt was poignant and somehow final.

It was I who had moved to the single bed, who had caused the separation, but the cost was high. I wanted a new life, though to claim it involved hurting someone else, and that brought a mountain of guilt. But then I fell in love with another man. Love was an imperative beyond my power to resist. After all, love *happens* to one, doesn't it? It is not something one chooses.

But of course I was choosing. I, who had felt dead, was suddenly in a chaotic moil of possibilities. It was as if little bits of myself had become dismembered. I lost any idea of who I was. Who was I? I followed every clue. I listened to anyone who might offer me advice. I became ridiculously open. I could have been led anywhere.

My diary of that time is full of bits of quoted wisdom, dreams, poems, love letters, telepathic moments, visions. I was obviously deeply impressed with myself. Certainly, there was not a grain of humor anywhere.

But we must take ourselves seriously when we're young. So much is at stake. Me, I was dealing with ghosts. All the "shouldn'ts" from my past were telling me what I was not allowed to do.

The whole world was reinvented when I fell madly in love. I was a gleeful child, taking everything for myself. I could say, "I want this." How delicious to demand satisfaction!

When I didn't get it, the world suddenly uninvented itself again.

A few years ago I met the surrealist painter Leonora Carrington in Mexico City. I had known her only as a dramatic young woman in a painting by the master surrealist of the twentieth century, Max Ernst. The painting is called *Leonora in the Morning Light,* and Leonora stares out at the viewer from a landscape of minotaurs, unicorns, and skeletons, herself an exotic dream creature suspended from a phallic vine.

The woman who sat across from me at her kitchen table was seventy-nine. Her gray hair was pulled back in a soft bun. Closing the window behind her against the strong wind, she joked that she didn't want to lose the little hair she had left. She wore slacks and sandals and I noticed the slight hump her back made beneath her sweater. As she passed me shots of tequila, we ate the spicy delicacy she had prepared from the black fungus that grows on corn. There was great humor and warmth in her eyes.

I was thinking about her recent sculptures, like dreams cast in bronze: a sphinx creature with a human held tenderly in its paws, a strange desolate god with a door that opened in its body and a horn protruding through its forehead.

She was proving to be one of those people whose

minds leap so fast that the sheer speed of their ideas makes them fun to be with. I was telling her about the opening scene in a novel I had just read, Timothy Findley's *Headhunter*. A woman sits in a reference library reading *Heart of Darkness*. She is one of the bag ladies, rubbies, and dopers for whom the library is the only port in a storm. As she reads she realizes in terror that she has released Conrad's evil character Kurtz from his jungle.

"Of course that happens," Leonora said. "Entities do exist. Have you never been occupied by an entity?"

A bit startled, I replied that I didn't think so.

"Just because you see someone as gifted doesn't mean they're not afraid," she said. "In fact the more gifted, the more afraid."

I didn't quite get the connection, but I think she was saying that, though I might not credit it, she too was fearful. I asked her, "Have you been occupied by entities?"

"Yes," she replied casually, "it has happened six or eight times since I was very young."

"What was it like?" I asked.

"It was a thing without shape or boundaries, amorphous. It came as a sound. It was voracious, a sucking force, and inside this entity were millions of other entities, equally voracious, crying desperately. Of which I was one. As in hell. And then it vomited me out."

Taken aback, I asked, "What was it?"

"It was female," she said. "It was inside. Voracious. Like Lilith who raged at the angels. Beneath us is this female anger and pain. Mountains of pain. We must deal with it."

I realized she was saying that this rage is in all of us.

Then she switched gears and told me she also believed in gods. "Jung was absolutely right about one thing," she remarked. "We are occupied by gods. The mistake is to identify with the god occupying you. Which god occupies you?" she asked me.

I began to see the playfulness behind her serious demeanor. These things she was talking about were psychological realities, though they were also cultural constructs. She was saying that, though we don't know it, we are always living myths.

"I've never thought of which god occupies me," I said.

"I would say Diana, the huntress."

"And you?" I asked.

"Demeter. I am occupied by the mother goddess. I am never free of my obsession with my children."

And then we began to talk of love. "The two genders," she said, "it must mean something. But never have I heard an adequate explanation of what the meeting of the sexes would mean. The kind of explanation where you say: Ah, yes!"

"You say 'would mean.' Have they not met?" I asked.

"Perhaps not, because, you see, we women are not ourselves. Men kick free," she said, "while women learn shame and fear. There is so much dogma turd, millennia of it to clear away. Once we were connected to the deep mysteries. We have lost so much of our original power."

And then she confessed: "What limits me is the fear of being alone. I mean alone when one is completely paralyzed. It is possible for a part of the soul to get lost, you know."

Leonora Carrington was born in Lancashire in 1917, the daughter of a textile tycoon. The family residence, Crookhey Hall, was run by a fleet of servants, and a Jesuit priest came on Sundays to give private mass in the family chapel. Her Irish mother was a remarkable beauty. When she took Leonora to make her debut at the court of King George V in 1934, she advised her rebellious young daughter to look "decorative" and added, "You'd better be careful or you'll be an old witch before you're twenty-five." That season, Leonora attended all the London balls, as well as the Royal Garden Party at Buckingham Palace. She watched the Ascot races from the Royal Enclosure. Her entrance into society was celebrated with a party at the Ritz.

After all that, Leonora decided she wanted to be a witch. She had been sent to finishing school in Florence, followed by school in Paris where she spent her time drawing and climbing out of windows to escape. Now, she persuaded her distraught parents to allow her to study art and enrolled at the Amédée Ozenfant Academy in London in 1936. A friend invited her to dinner with Max Ernst, a married man of forty-six. The encounter was electric.

In his surrealist writings and paintings, Ernst called

himself "Loplop, the Bird Superior." He was looking for his equal, his "bride of the wind." Leonora was perfect. She was young, beautiful, and, with what he called her innocent perversity, an exacting muse. She might have sprung from one of his own dreams. For her, he was the mentor/lover. He gave her recognition and praise and a way to rebel against family. He gave her access to a professional career. Because of him, her paintings would be included in the major International Surrealist Exhibition in France in 1937.

The lovers moved to Paris, where Leonora soon found herself embattled with Ernst's second wife, Marie-Berthe Aurenche, though that ten-year marriage was already floundering. After squabbles, separations, and reunions, Leonora and Ernst finally settled in the south of France, where they found a farmhouse in the village of Saint-Martin d'Ardèche. Ernst returned to Paris that winter to sort out what Leonora called his "genital responsibilities." "I didn't think he'd ever come back, I didn't know where I was going. I was like a monster. At least I felt like some sort of performing animal, a bear with a ring in its nose. I was l'Anglaise." But Ernst did return. They decorated the outside of their house with household gods and goddesses with fish, horse, and bird heads and painted the inside walls and furniture. Leonora wrote fantastical stories to Ernst that novelist Marina Warner calls "at once naive and perverse, comic and lethal." They treated everything as play. "It was," Leonora recalled, "an era of paradise."

On September 1, 1939, France declared war on Germany. Even though he had been living in the country for fifteen years, Max Ernst was arrested as an enemy alien and sent to a detainment camp. At Leonora's instigation, friends lobbied and secured his release. Months later, denounced by a villager as a German spy, he was rearrested. He escaped and returned to Saint-Martin, only to be caught again and sent back to prison camp. As she tried desperately to free him, Leonora began to suffer a nervous breakdown. She stopped eating and was hallucinating. Friends convinced her she must flee to Spain.

When Ernst was finally released and returned to Saint-Martin, he found Leonora gone. He stayed on and painted obsessively. Despair fueled his work. (Even in the prison camps he never stopped painting.) He produced two of his most famous paintings, *Leonora in the Morning Light* and *Europe After the Rain*.

The Nazis had publicly denounced him as a degenerate artist, an enemy of the Reich, and it was imperative for him to get out of France. He went to Marseilles, where coincidence brought him into contact with the rich American heiress Peggy Guggenheim. With her entourage, he traveled to Lisbon, where she had a plane standing by.

Leonora had also made it to Spain, but as she crossed the border she had begun to spiral out of control. Diagnosed by doctors as incurably insane, she was institutionalized. She underwent shock and drug therapy that was so horrendous she came to call it the "death practice." When the British Embassy finally informed her parents of their daughter's condition, they dispatched her old nanny to collect her. The two women made their way to Lisbon. Convinced the family's intention was to ship her to a sanatorium in South Africa, Leonora managed to escape from a restaurant by climbing out a washroom window. She fled to the Mexican Embassy, where an acquaintance, the poet Renato Leduc, worked as a diplomat. He agreed to marry her so that she could get a visa to the United States.

Max Ernst and Peggy Guggenheim had also arrived in Lisbon, and by now they were lovers. Though Ernst wanted to resume his affair with Leonora, she refused.

The couples traveled separately to New York. Ernst lived with Guggenheim while Leonora lived with Leduc. At the end of the summer of 1942, five years after their first meeting, Leonora moved to Mexico, which was offering citizenship to refugees from the resistance movements. Shortly thereafter, she and Leduc dissolved their marriage of convenience. She never saw Max Ernst again.

Established in an apartment in Mexico City, Leonora wrote the whole experience of her flight in a harrowing story called "Down Below." (When I asked, she assured me the story was autobiographical.) It is possibly one of the most lucidly hallucinatory accounts of madness that has been written. "At least when you go mad you find out what you are made of," she said laconically.

For decades, in any record of Max Ernst's life, Leonora

was a brief interlude; in hers, he was the stumbling block, one of the "death practices" that she had had to survive. Fascinated interviewers would return obsessively to those Ernst years, thereby unintentionally diminishing her own work.

In *Significant Others*, a book of essays about how intimate partnerships affect creativity, Susan Suleiman writes a wonderful essay about Ernst and Carrington. Leonora, she suggests, had unwittingly taken on the role closest to the heart of the male surrealists, that of the *femme-enfant*, the child-woman or inspired madwoman who brought erotic play to their art. Leonora herself said the surrealists' women were assigned the role of the "slightly crazy muse." There were positive and negative aspects to this assignment. Leonora had found in Ernst all the performers at once—"mentor, lover (both faithful and faithless), idealized father, and artistic brother in arms." She was empowered, and then she was overwhelmed.

In the view of the more brutal outsiders, she had parlayed her beauty into professional opportunities. She had entered a familiar story in which success for a woman was to be sexually desired by a successful man. Had she stayed with Ernst, she would have risked being absorbed. What is precocious is how clearly she understood this.

"Leonora [was] the only woman Max had ever loved." At least that's what Peggy Guggenheim believed. In New York, Ernst tried to persuade Leonora to stay with him, but Guggenheim said she refused. "She felt that her life with Max was over because she could no longer be his slave, and that was the only way she could live with him." She needed to leave him to find her own art.

According to his son, Ernst was devastated by Leonora's abandonment: "I don't recall ever again seeing such a strange mixture of desolation and euphoria in my father's face [as] when he returned from his first meeting with Leonora in New York. ... Each day that he saw her, and it was often, ended the same way. I hoped never to experience such pain myself."

Painful though it may have been, Leonora had the courage to walk away. Hers becomes a story about recognizing one's choices. She was not destroyed. She married a photographer and had two children and a number of grandchildren. She is now regarded as one of Mexico's most important artists, indeed a national treasure.

24

I Want This

She hated the world with its calm assurance of purpose. It was all a ruin. She had staked everything. Everything for Nothing.

The end of a love affair is bitter. We feel as though life itself has failed us.

I remember when I found the inevitable letter in the mailbox at the end of my lane. I walked into the woods and opened it. The pain, as Elizabeth Smart would have said, lit up the sky like lightning. It is hard not to dismiss this with irony: the rejection by a lover seems trivial when placed against the world's suffering. But it must be accorded its dignity. Such emotional pain plunges one to the bottom of one's own need, which is the first necessary step in the construction of the compassionate self.

All those needs, unclaimed and projected onto others, are the crude basis for the world's murderousness. To my astonishment, I found the following entry in my diary of that time:

I sit here with the smell of spruce at my back and for a moment I can imagine how the psyche turns murderous. Too much apartness, too much failure, and an insane distaste takes over. What would it be to eliminate these trivial little human machines? It's a very impersonal irrationality. Not anger, but dismissive disgust. They're so ridiculous in their capacity to survive. And everything that might be beautiful and pull you back into life is only silly, pointless and finally hostile.

After what I took to be the failure of all love, I had come to hate human beings.

It took a year of tramping the streets of London to come to terms with my own self-deception. I had bought all the romantic propaganda and, even after the affair was over, continued to insist that one particular man was what I needed for my life, and when he would not conform to my version of him, I could not imagine how to go on. Without him, I was destroyed.

In retrospect, I believe that the year of loneliness in London was more important than the love affair. Slowly and painfully, I discovered the word *tolerance*. I had to tolerate the fact that life had other plans for me. (And they turned out to be more interesting than any I could have invented at the time.) I had to give up the willful fantasy not only that I could control another person but even that I could control my own life.

Obsessive love is a training ground. My lesson was quite simple—how to say "I want this," something I hadn't been able to do before. In the end it didn't matter whether I got the object of my desire or not. In the end, in fact, I was lucky I didn't, because I never really knew the man independent of my idea of him. When obsessive passion is over and the projections are ripped away, the person standing there is almost always a stranger. For romantic love *is* projection—projection of all that is most dramatic, indeed lovely, and unclaimable in the self.

Years later I found myself back in the city where I had fallen in love. As I drove through the streets, I laughed. I felt such an affectionate humor at the intensity of that younger self caught up in all that pain and grief. As the playwright August Strindberg once said, "Ah, the agony of ecstasy and the ecstasy of agony. You look for love outside yourself when love is your very nature."

There will come a time when all the love letters, written in such anguish, will become simply words on a page. A signature that once brought a shock to your heart will be mere ink. Sadness will be a vague memory. But never say the love affair was trivial. It will always be one of the most important experiences of your life. This is how we learn the dimensions of our own desire.

Coda: The Story Resumes

Women of the Heart

The problem was simply getting out of bed. The sheer will it took to plant one foot on the floor and then the other, to haul herself up, to breathe in and out. To keep at it.

She took a job waiting tables in a posh French restaurant in the city's gay district. Why did they say *waiting tables?* You never waited. You rushed around filling people's mouths. To them, you were invisible. Just a conveyor belt passing food from kitchen to tables. But at least she didn't have to think what to do with her nights.

And she felt at home here. Waiters and waitresses were interesting people. Most were out-of-work actors, writers, filmmakers, on their way somewhere else. Putting in time till they got to do what they really wanted to do. Like her, they were the walking wounded.

Time off was hardest. She was haunted. He was there in front of her on the street where he couldn't possibly be: a familiar profile, the way a shoulder tilted under the weight of a reclining head. She was ashamed to admit she'd kept the candied skull. Macabre. The touch was enough to bring back his hand holding it, holding her.

She had cut people out of her life. She preferred plants. On her days off, she went to the Palm House, a domed and winged pavilion of glass like an island salvaged from the urban decay around it. The homeless drunks and the drug pushers hid out here, but they weren't threatening. They were all broken.

She thought of it as the garden temple. It was possible to enter its heavy wet heat and be somewhere else. She loved the names of the plants: ixora, flame of the woods, with its fists of orange flowers; clivia, the duchess with leather-strap leaves and orange trumpet-shaped blossoms slipping from its cracks; acalypha, its long red plumes hanging like a chenille fringe. Her favorite was the sensitive plant, *Mimosa pudica*, with its delicate fronds like piano fingers. The slightest touch and it recoiled and folded itself up. It was a fraud, really, not delicate at all. One of the toughest survivors in the greenhouse, it rooted itself in the least bit of soil.

How do you do endings? she wondered. She suddenly realized she could do this forever, manage on the memory of a ghost. For a long time her deepest emotional life went on elsewhere, in a phantom place.

Nursing a broken heart. She imagined filling the hole in her chest with gauze bandages. Stuffing it, stuffing it until she couldn't breathe.

She needed to get out of the city. A trip somewhere, anywhere. To Mexico. She was telling herself she wanted to see the city again. Back to the Gran Hotel where they remembered her; they were so friendly it was almost as though they'd missed her. How beautiful the Zócalo was with its cathedral sinking slowly into the Aztec ruins that lay under its foundations. Six months and nothing had changed. She waited until the day before she was due to leave before she called him.

He sounded surprised and yet grateful. "You've been in the city seven days? How could you have waited so long?" he chided. She could feel her hands shake, her palms go cold and damp as she heard the familiar timbre of his voice.

They arranged to meet at the Zapata. He was sitting at a back table, a thin man in a jean jacket with a sad face now covered in a black beard. She thought, He's all wrong. But then he looked up and she did a double-take—the same hot clutch at the heart, the weakness in the knees, the delicious sense of surrender.

They talked carefully at first, bringing each other up to date. She was working in a restaurant. She was doing some writing. He said he'd given up painting. His brother was starting a franchise in San Francisco, and he was going to be the importer of Mexican crafts. She'd forgotten he had a brother. Or had he even told her? Maybe it was just that she hadn't wanted to know he had a normal anything. Not a brother or a sister, just a life as *her* lover.

He wanted to know why they'd hurt each other. But he was busy with his life. He said this as an afterthought, to console her. Her first impulse was to defend herself: How had she hurt him? But what was the point? The words shriveled up. There was nothing more to say.

Back at her hotel she asked herself for the umpteenth time: what had that all been about? Did men love differently from women? Didn't they get obsessed too? Yes, she thought bitterly, but life gives them more options.

In Toronto nothing much changed. She still worked nights, but slowly the two-dimensional, black-and-white world began to take on faint color. She forced herself to go to parties, though she always felt she was up for an audition, some man deciding whether she would get the part. She took yoga, she started Spanish lessons, she kept busy. She had materialized the ghost, seen him in the flesh, and he was real. But had she really exorcised the phantom in her head?

One night she found herself watching that old tear-jerker *Casablanca*. She'd forgotten how powerful it was. A voice saying, "A story of an imperishable love and the enthralling saga of six desperate people, each in Casablanca to keep an appointment with destiny." She loved the look of Humphrey Bogart as Rick, the sensitive but hard-nosed hero running a gin joint. His insides had been kicked out when he was left standing on a train platform in Paris. The only woman in the world he'd ever loved and she chose his gin joint to walk into in Casablanca. And Ingrid Bergman as Ilsa, with that luminous quality in her face, her eyes back-lit with longing. She was in love with Rick, but Victor, head of the French Resistance, needed her.

It occurred to her that most of the great love stories take place in wartime. You had to have something worth sacrificing to the greater cause. What you sacrificed was love.

She watched the film's trailer. It turns out that in the great airport scene, the airplane was a cardboard cut-out and the actors hired to play the mechanics were all midgets to keep everything to scale. Until the very last minute the screenwriters didn't know how they were going to end the film. Ingrid Bergman kept asking: "Who do I go off with?"

It must be the most famous final dialogue in cinema:

Rick: You're getting on that plane with Victor where you belong. ... You're part of his work, the thing that keeps him going. ... If that plane leaves the ground and you're not with him, you'll always regret it. Maybe not today, maybe not tomorrow, but soon and for the rest of your life.

Ilsa: But what about us?

Rick: We'll always have Paris ...

Ilsa: When I said I would never leave you.

Rick: And you never will. But I've got a job to do too. Where I'm going you can't follow. What I've got to do you can't be any part of.

As always, she thought, *he* gets to choose for *her*. He tells her somebody else needs her and then he goes off with his buddy, saying, "I think this is the beginning of a beautiful friendship."

She laughed now. "Stupid Fucker." She was thinking about Michael Ondaatje writing his Bogart suite of poems. Rick, six months later, lying drunk in a hotel and seeing "the stupidity of his gesture."

> Stupid fucker
> he says to himself, stupid fucker
> and knocks the bottle
> leaning against his bare stomach
> onto the sheet. Gin stems
> out like a four leaf clover.
> I used to be lucky he says
> I had white suits black friends
> who played the piano.

She realized she hadn't been broken at all. That's what

happened in films and poems. That was the story. But the person writing it was having a good time.

She'd been using love to avoid loneliness. She'd wanted the big transformation, but there were no fast tracks. At least, she thought, being alone you could begin to find out what was in you. These past weeks she'd kept dreaming of babies: babies with little blue legs barely able to stand; babies like tiny gerbils she could hold in her hand. She'd spent enough time roiling around in her own psyche to know what that meant. Something inside had changed; something small and consequential was growing. A small beginning. That's what she wanted now.

She made a commitment to herself: she wouldn't ever hang her needs on a ghost. Her lovers would be real flesh and blood; her fantasies were her own property. Of course she wanted to be with someone, but that could wait. Right now, the possibility of taking charge of her life was heady enough.

Afterword

After reading this book in manuscript, a friend said, "Now you've ripped away my illusions, what's left? I'm in mourning." We laughed, but she was half serious.

Why, we asked each other, are women afraid of giving up the fantasy of obsessive love? Is it because we think we will be left with nothing?

But everything is to be gained! There's a film that's such a perfect allegory of romantic obsession that it should be compulsory viewing—Anthony Minghella's *Truly, Madly, Deeply*. A young woman's husband dies suddenly. She is devastated, haunted by his memory, unable to imagine how to resume her life. He was a cellist. When her sister asks to use his cello, she reacts hysterically. She feels violated, as if someone had asked for his body. It is at this point that he returns, literally, as a ghost and takes up residence in her house.

At first, he is the perfect idealization that she mourns. But soon he does the things he did in life. He brings home his ghost friends to play Bach concertos, turning her into his audience. She's the desperate one again. "Don't be long," she says, as she slips off to bed. He takes over her flat as he once did her life. He and his fellow spooks turn up the heat, strip the floors, and rearrange the furniture. She's got spooks watching television in her bedroom, and yet *she's* the one accused of being unreasonable. Finally, she explodes. It's a wonderful moment. For the first time she is as real, ironically, as he is. She remembers how much she gave away, all the things she buried in trunks out of sight because he disapproved, how she deferred because she wanted to be the perfect lover. Now she realizes it's life she wants—her life.

At the end, the film plays with the viewer. Is the ghost husband a figment of her imagination? Or has he returned to free her of the idealized phantom she has made him into? No matter. She recovers him as a flawed, endearing human being whom she deeply loved. And, she can finally let him go.

In that first, devastating suffering at the end of a love affair, when our obsession is ripped from us, we must learn that all that passion, all that wonderful ferment in the psyche, all that love is in us, and the only question is how to use it in the world. Of course we'll fall in love again. But there are many kinds of love waiting for us.

I'm trying to find a way to speak of self-worth without falling into all those clichés that so trivialize the notion, that seem little more than the ego taking a warm bath. I found a lovely passage in the diary of Virginia Woolf: "I came to have a deep feeling of my own importance. Not in relation to human beings, in relation to the force which had respected me sufficiently to make me feel what was real."

Life is mysterious. And difficult. We need a clear-eyed awareness of the illusions by which we live. We need the resilience to survive the continuous shattering of our fondest ideas of ourselves. But if there is anything that makes life exciting, it's the sense of inquiry, the ongoing discovery. In exhilarating flashes, we see, if only for moments, what it is we're up to.

What women most deeply want, if we only knew it, is to take charge of the love story; to arrange not to depend on love but to embrace it fully when it comes. The pitfalls are these: self-pity, shutting down the self, settling for safety.

Let's go back to Aristophanes' hermaphrodite. Do we really want a matching other? One of the richest pleasures of a relationship is the capacity to accord each other solitude. Not possessive attachment. There must be enough oxygen, enough space to breathe. To be cherished, to be accompanied—yes, that's what we want. To be intimately, physically entwined with another. Yes. But not the old fantasy: *We are one.* Let there be separateness and balance: two resourceful people greeting, face to face.

For those who have the stamina to learn the lessons of obsessive passion, romantic love can turn into something more real and durable, into a commitment with deep roots, in which each person accepts, even celebrates, the fallible, imperfect other. How do we get this? By offering it and demanding it back. By settling for nothing less.

Acknowledgments

Part of the pleasure in completing a book is the opportunity to thank all those who have supported one in the process of writing it.

First, and most importantly, I would like to thank my editor, Iris Tupholme, who believed in this book and convinced me I could write it. Her incisive editing, good humor, and unfailing generosity make her a writer's delight. Thanks also to Alberto Manguel who, in the early stages of my obsession with this subject, invited me to apply for a residency fellowship at the Banff Centre for the Arts; to Don Obe who edited my first article on romantic love; and to Cassandra Pybus, who published that article.

A special thanks is due to my friend and reader, Arlene Lampert, who is always there for me, and to Marlene

Goldman and Richard Teleky, whose sharp and incisive comments on the manuscript were invaluable.

I would also like to express my gratitude to Sharon Sullivan, Colleen Sullivan, Patricia Cress, Laurie Maher, Tara Maher, Phyllis Bruce, Kitty Hoffman, and María Teresa Larraín, who read the manuscript and offered helpful suggestions. To those who have offered me inspiration on the subject I extend my thanks: Jeni Couzyn, Anne Michaels, P.K. Page, Leon Whiteson, Mark Levene, Elizabeth Harvey, and Amélia Jimenez. I would also like to thank Jennifer Bates for her assistance in translating the extract from "Autumn Day," by Rainer Marie Rilke. Thanks to Bill Hubacheck of the Revue Video for making his extensive film collection available to me; to Derek Vincent who knows so much about videography; and to Tina Meale at the Film Reference Library, the Toronto International Film Festival Group.

I would like to commend the high professionalism of my copy editor Shaun Oakey, and that of Nicole Langlois and Ian Murray and of all the editorial staff at HarperCollins Canada. I owe a great deal to my agents, Jan Whitford and Jackie Kaiser, whose support for my work has been so crucial. And finally, to my partner Juan Opitz, who has taught me so much, I extend my love.

Editions consulted include: Gustave Flaubert, *Madame Bovary*, translated by Geoffrey Wall (London: Penguin Classics, 1992); Dante Alighieri, *La Vita Nuova*, translated

by Barbara Reynolds (London: Penguin Classics, 1969);
Plato, *Symposium: The Collected Dialogues*, translated by Edith
Hamilton and Huntington Cairns (New York: Pantheon,
Bollingen Series LXXI, 1961); Boris Pasternak, *Doctor
Zhivago*, translated by Max Hayward and Manya Harari
(New York: Pantheon, 1991); Johann Wolfgang von
Goethe, *The Sorrows of Young Werther*, translated by Michael
Hulse (London: Penguin Classics, 1989); Marguerite
Duras, *The Lover*, translated by Barbara Bray (New York:
Random House, 1985); and Daphne du Maurier, *Rebecca*
(New York: Random House, 1993). The extract from
Alice Munro is taken from "Bardon Bus" in *The Moons of
Jupiter* (Toronto: Macmillan Canada, 1982).

The quotation from the poem "Tin Roof" by Michael
Ondaatje is used with the author's permission. (He
explained that the hotel in which Rick is drunk is to be
found in Anton Chekov's story "The Lady with the Dog.")

Quotations from Elizabeth Smart's *By Grand Central
Station I Sat Down and Wept* and from *The Journals of Elizabeth
Smart* are used by permission of Sebastian Barker.